Diary of a Low-Born Cleric

MICHAEL COREN

Diary of a Low-Born Cleric

A Year in the Priesthood

DUNDURN PRESS

Publisher and acquiring editor: Meghan Macdonald | Editor: Russell Smith
Cover designer: Karen Alexiou
Cover image: church: Karsten Winegeart/Unsplash; sky: H&CO/Unsplash

Library and Archives Canada Cataloguing in Publication

Title: Diary of a low-born cleric : a year in the priesthood / Michael Coren.
Names: Coren, Michael, author
Identifiers: Canadiana (print) 20250247615 | Canadiana (ebook) 20250247623 | ISBN 9781459755949 (softcover) | ISBN 9781459755963 (EPUB) | ISBN 9781459755956 (PDF)
Subjects: LCSH: Coren, Michael—Diaries. | LCSH: Anglican Church of Canada—Clergy—Biography. | LCGFT: Diaries. | LCGFT: Autobiographies.
Classification: LCC BX5620.C654 A3 2026 | DDC 283.092—dc23

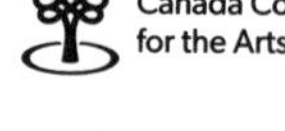

We acknowledge the support of the Canada Council for the Arts and the Ontario Arts Council for our publishing program. We also acknowledge the financial support of the Government of Ontario, through the Ontario Book Publishing Tax Credit and Ontario Creates, and the Government of Canada.

Printed and bound in Canada.

Dundurn Press
1382 Queen Street East
Toronto, Ontario, Canada M4L 1C9
dundurn.com, @dundurnpress

To Moss and Lyla

Introduction

First, a little about the title. In 1170 an infamous martyrdom took place in southern England, perhaps the most infamous in British history. Thomas Becket, Archbishop of Canterbury, was slaughtered in his cathedral by a group of knights sent by King Henry II. The notorious line that has come down to us has monarch Henry shouting, "Will no one rid me of this turbulent priest?"

Very grand, very much the stuff of history, and very likely not accurate. What he probably said was something closer to "What miserable drones and traitors have I nurtured and promoted in my household who let their lord be treated with such shameful contempt by a low-born cleric!" This refers to the fact that Becket had been born in Cheapside in London rather than in a palace or castle, and that while his parents, Gilbert and Matilda, were minor gentry and owned property, they and their son were hardly elite. That would have been more than enough to qualify them as low-born.

Stung and humiliated by such words of rebuke, and likely encouraged by plenty of wine, four of Henry's knights rode off to do the business. They found Thomas by the High Altar at Canterbury Cathedral, and after some rather aggressive verbal exchanges — in which the archbishop, with some "low-born" toughness, gave as good as he got — they attacked him. Perhaps they intended assault rather than murder, but drunken anger does tend to get out of control, and they ended up slicing him across the top of his head, opening his skull, and spilling his brains on the floor. One of them then said, with all of the subtlety and delicacy expected of early medieval thugs, "We can leave this place, knights, he will not get up again."

He didn't.

It wasn't very long before he was regarded as a martyr. Some of the abbey monks, accompanied by the wonderfully named Ernold the Goldsmith, understood the unenviable task of mopping up Becket's brains and then keeping them safe in a basin. His body was then moved to the crypt and protected behind large, locked doors. Three months later the crypt was opened to the public and suddenly various miracles occurred, all attributed to the slaughtered archbishop. More than seven hundred were soon documented, with pilgrims, and even those who merely prayed to Becket from further afield, claiming that they had been cured of leprosy, blindness, epilepsy, and pretty much everything else that plagued the country. The news reached Rome, and in February 1173, Pope Alexander III proclaimed Becket a saint. As a consequence, the place of his martyrdom became one of Europe's major destinations for Christian pilgrimage. King Henry himself eventually had to perform public penance, and Becket has come down to us in books, legends, movies, and in the names of countless churches.

I'm not altogether sympathetic to the man, brave as he was in his final moments. He was made an archbishop because his friend the king assumed that he'd be malleable and obedient. He changed, perhaps underwent something like a conversion, and instead defended the rights of the church against those of the crown. But he defended the church as an institution rather than the faith, and I've a problem with that. We see it even today, when people really should know that institutions will always let us down, even those centred around sacred teachings. However, this is a sort of diary rather than a sort of history book, so enough about the twelfth century.

I have no intention of ever being put into a Becket-like situation or anything like it — I hope to die in my bed surrounded by single-malt whisky and very good milk chocolate — but I'll take "low-born cleric" as a title any day. Because in many ways and to many people, that is what I am. My father was a taxi-driver in London, the son of Jewish immigrants from eastern Europe, and was raised in a rough part of town. Mum was from the East End of London, yards away from where Jack the Ripper committed his ghastly murders. Both my parents left school early, both were brilliant, and neither was given the opportunities that they deserved.

I've been much more fortunate. Or, as I prefer to say, blessed. And blessings are something I've tried to record in this diary of a clerical year. But when I speak of blessings, I don't mean only the joy and love and pleasure resulting from being a priest but also the challenges and difficulties and even pain associated with the clerical life. It's not always easy, and if anybody says otherwise, they almost certainly have no idea what's involved. However, I can't write an honest personal diary without also writing about my life as a journalist. I am what is apparently known as "bi-vocational," which sounded far sexier when I first heard it. I write books, I write columns for numerous Canadian and British newspapers and magazines, and I sometimes appear on television and radio.

Not as much of the latter as I used to, but for more than fifteen years I hosted nightly shows. I'm still recognized because of them, and more than once have heard, "Didn't you used to be Michael Coren?"

My interlocutors have a point. You see, ordination changes someone, as it is supposed to do, and I hope I'm a different person for all sorts of reasons. Nonetheless, for me there's a symbiotic relationship between the priesthood and journalism. I'm given a public platform in media to preach the Gospel just as in church I've a literal pulpit. Also, my life and experience as a priest now form the basis for my writing, and my ability as a cleric to reach out to people is broadened and deepened by my functioning in public life and in media. As priests, however, we must never, ever become the centre of attention because the centre, the divine epicentre, is Jesus. All we can do is point the way, and if ever we forget that, we're in deep trouble. I hope I haven't forgotten that in this diary and that therefore it reveals how I live my calling.

My life isn't sufficiently interesting to be the subject of a conventional diary; nor is this a strict and rigid daily recording of my activities. I chose the year 2024 not because it was unique or even special but precisely because it wasn't. It was just like any other year for me. I of course write about my life and activities in 2024 but spin off into discussions of what else has happened, historically and theologically, on particular days or weeks. We are never alone, and need to understand and listen to the past, grasp the context and foundation of our lives. Be steady on that stepping stone as you cross the water; otherwise, you may topple and fall. Become steady by understanding what has gone before you.

Regarding the diary's order and chronology, the church year actually begins on the first Sunday of Advent, which is in early December. I considered beginning this book about a year in the life of a priest on that date but thought that might be a little too insular. For most people, including most Christians if we're honest, the first day of January marks the beginning of the new year. So to the purists: I ask your forgiveness. To the pedants: Do your worst. To the rest of you: I hope you enjoy this book.

I should say that some names in this book have been changed because themes are discussed that are personal and painful. Even when names have been changed, I've always asked permission to include the stories. Otherwise, I've been candid and open, even raw at times, and that might not be to everybody's taste. Church life, the Christian life, may be many things, but it's not and never will be to everybody's taste. It's not comfort food — not if it's authentic. I don't have many exceptional qualities, but I do pride myself on my authenticity.

January

January 1

I've never kept a new year's resolution in my life. There's so much pressure to stick to what you decide that keeping it is almost impossible. I suppose my hope for the coming year is that we'll see the dignity in those people we so often ignore or even reject, hear the compelling stories of people we've never bothered to listen to, and realize that the opposite of being "woke" is to be asleep in the face of loneliness, marginalization, and pain. Gustave Flaubert, whose novel *Madame Bovary* remains one of the finest works in the French language, once said, "It is true that I am endowed with an absurd sensitiveness, what scratches others tears me to pieces." He was mocked for that comment, considered self-praising and precious. In fact, he was being boldly candid. Such candour made his writing memorable, and it's what can transform our world.

January 2

The truth is that I've always found January slightly depressing, something of an anticlimax after the festivities of Christmas. I realize that the Christmas season continues after the big day, but the emotional highs of childhood are difficult to forget, and I find that the older I get, the more I recall the delights of former days. It's also close to the date when my father died, and while we didn't have a bad relationship, I don't think I ever understood or fully appreciated him. I never properly told him how grateful I was for all that he'd done and sacrificed and if I'm honest with myself, I didn't show him enough respect. I don't mean anything formal but just an implicit acknowledgement of his worth and dignity. I suppose that's not uncommon for children and until I became a dad myself, I didn't realize how demanding fatherhood was, but I still feel a ripple of guilt each January.

Telling others how you feel about them is so vital, especially when people are close to the end of their lives, either at home or in hospital. Recently I gave communion to a terribly ill woman, and after a few moments of prayer, I asked her if she needed anything else. "No," she said, "I'm fine. I've had my time, a wonderful husband who loved me, a fabulous family, lots of friends, and I've been able to tell all those close to me that I love them. I've been able to say thank you. Because of that I'm at peace." Then she smiled, held my hand, and thanked me. She died the following morning. I was the last person to give her the sacrament.

• • •

A young mum came to see me to inquire about the church and ask about what we believe and what we expected of her. Most of her questions were straightforward, enthusiastic, and easy to answer. I assured her that yes, her children would be most welcome and not to worry about any noise they made. I shared a story of a priest preaching in a church with a mother and baby in the front pew. Suddenly the mum got up with her child and went to leave. "No, don't go," said the priest, "he's not disturbing me." "No," she replied, "but you're disturbing him."

She laughed, all was going grandly, and she then asked about the availability of an alternative form of host. I assumed she was going to ask for one that was gluten-free and that I could smugly explain that we did indeed have those and that we were always extremely sensitive to our congregational needs. "No," she said, "I'm fine with gluten but it's my daughter. She really doesn't like the flavour of the ones she usually gets and wondered if you do them in any others." For one of the first times in my life I was genuinely speechless. All those years of seminary and this never came up. Yet another crisis in modern Christianity.

I was supposed to be in Israel and Palestine right now, but my trip was cancelled because of the conflict around Gaza. I've spent a great deal of time in the region, once lived there for almost a year, but there's one particular incident that has never left me. It was during an especially dangerous period for suicide bombing, people in both communities were frightened, and I was travelling from Bethlehem back into Israel, about the only non-local to be doing so at that time. In front of me a Palestinian grandfather and his grandson were arguing with a soldier behind the security barrier. I could follow some but not all of the conversation. Then, suddenly, the little boy lifted up his shirt to reveal a package taped to him. I remember thinking, *It's a bomb. This is madness. What a ridiculous place to die.* Others obviously came to the same conclusion because alarms went off, soldiers rushed forward, and then there was silence. It was a colostomy bag, and the grandfather had been arguing about his out-of-date papers preventing him from taking his grandson to a Jerusalem hospital. An officer came forward, opened the barrier, and let the boy and his grandfather through. "Good luck," he said in Hebrew. "Thank you," said the man in Arabic. The situation in the region is obviously far more complicated than this story suggests, and I know it well enough not to be naive or even too optimistic, but beyond the clashing, tearing narratives there is still humanity in the depths of suffering. I've seen it shine repeatedly in the last places it would be expected, and I still cling to the essential Christian hope and pray that somehow the Holy Land can be made the place it ought to be.

January 5

January is the season of Epiphany, which for Christians is the manifestation of Jesus to the gentiles in the person of the Magi. In secular terms, an epiphany is a revelation, a transformation, a new way of seeing things, which is something I pray for regularly regarding Israel and Palestine. If only there could be a new understanding, a sweeping, overwhelming sense of realization, a shockingly new perception. Will that ever happen? Who knows! I remember a joke I was told when I first visited Israel. A man is praying by the Kotel, the Western Wall, the Wailing Wall, the holiest spot in Judaism, when a passerby approaches him.

Passerby: "Do you come and pray often in this extraordinary place?"

Praying man: "Every single day."

Passerby: "What do you pray for?"

Praying man: "For peace in the region, for Israelis and Palestinians to live in harmony, and for love to replace hatred in the world."

Passerby: "Forgive my cynicism, but we seem to be going in the opposite direction. Do you ever feel it's a waste of time?"

Praying man: "Waste of time? Sometimes I think I'm speaking to a brick wall!"

The specific feast day of Epiphany is marked on January 6, but the season itself runs until late February. January 6 commemorates the visit of the three wise men, those gentile Magi, to see the baby

Jesus in Bethlehem. It's the twelfth day after Christmas and is all about the wonder, mystery, and the miracle of seeing God made human in the most vulnerable form: that of a tiny baby. It also closes the Christmas season, which is where we get the idea of Twelfth Night, on January 5.

Those people who lament the hedonism of Christmas may not appreciate that in medieval Europe, Christmas was a period of heavy drinking, over-eating, and extended partying, which came to a head on Twelfth Night. The alcoholic punch consumed at Christmas was called "wassail"; it was made of cider, wine, and ale, often mulled with spices. Medieval revellers would consume the stuff in vast quantities as they gathered in homes or travelled from door to door, wishing the best to their neighbours and drinking to a good harvest. The word "wassail" likely has its origins in *ves heill*, Old Norse meaning "be in good health." It wasn't specifically linked to drinking at first, but wassail often became "drinkhail," and by the seventeenth century was associated with Christmas, Christmas Eve, and Twelfth Night. There were also particular cakes and pastries, such as the tortell and king cake, baked on Twelfth Night itself. Various other foods came along as the season evolved, with turkey a regular on the Christmas table as early as the sixteenth century. As well as turkey there was chicken, beef, and goose and sometimes swan and peacock. Cranberry sauce with swan or peacock? Surely not.

There's an entire debate to be had about the Christmas tree, the date of the holiday, and pretty much everything else associated with this time of year. In parts of the Hispanic world, there are parades and fancy-dress parties on Twelfth Night. Today, people dress as Spiderman as often as they do Biblical characters, but the idea of adventure and celebration is still there. In Bulgaria, people dive into freezing cold rivers to search for crucifixes that have been thrown into the water, and those who find them are said to be safe from evil spirits for the rest of the year. Let's hope the ritual also cures them of pneumonia.

In the Anglican church we're slightly less demonstrative and hardy than that, preferring a glass of sherry and a good chat. The point is that those who insist that we "Remember the Reason for the Season" and lament what Christmas has become have a somewhat distorted view of the history of the holiday.

But all this fun and joy can lead to a post-Christmas crisis, especially after the new year. January can be an intensely difficult time for people who suffer from genuine depression or have experienced recent loss. Leaving church today, I ask an elderly man, full of life if a little unsteady on his feet, how he's doing. "Quite well, thank you," he says, dignified and alert. "The problem is that I've reached an age where all of my friends are gone. I'm the last one. And I'm so damned lonely." I've heard it before, this cry of isolation, being alone when everybody else seems surrounded by friends and family. It's one of the successes of the church that we can bring people together who would otherwise have no point of contact with others, but it's only a small dent in the problem, this plague of unseen pain and anguish. I take the man to the pub where I listen to his stories from his childhood and youth in Britain, and we both moan that the beer is too cold.

January 13

There are numerous feast days and holy days in the Anglican, Roman Catholic, and Eastern Orthodox church calendars. The more Protestant churches aren't so keen on these as they rely on the Bible alone. They believe that traditions that evolved outside of scripture aren't accurate. We Anglicans are more permissive, and the different traditions within Anglicanism place a higher or lower emphasis on some of the special days. January 1, for example, is the feast of the circumcision of Jesus. He was Jewish, so circumcised on the eighth day after his birth. Luke's Gospel tells us, "And when the eight days were accomplished for the circumcising of the child, his name was called Jesus, which was so named of the angel before he was conceived in the womb." That we've no idea whether his birthday was December 25 — it likely wasn't — means his bris, the ritual circumcision, was probably not January 1, but chronological accuracy isn't what is being acknowledged.

My "ceremony" was also in January and thank God I've no memory of it. I was told many years later that my father got drunk, my mother cried, and someone almost got into a fight with the *mohel*, the person who performs the circumcision. It might say something about my life that I had a bris but not a bar mitzvah, during which a thirteen-year-old receives gifts, money, and praise after reading from the Bible in a synagogue. The agony without the ecstasy: there was no rejoicing, gifts, or dancing for me. It was my own fault, because I insisted to my father that I didn't want to continue with my morning Hebrew classes. Because my maternal grandma wasn't born Jewish, I was only tenuously qualified anyway, but a party would have brightened up my early teens, when I seemed to be constantly embarrassed about me, girls, people, me, and girls.

January 15

Today is my birthday. I was born this day in 1959, exactly four hundred years after the coronation of Queen Elizabeth I. Not her accession to the throne, which took place on November 17, 1558, but her coronation on the date chosen by her personal astrologer, John Dee. It's fashionable to criticize Queen Elizabeth, largely because she's been so revered and respected over the centuries. If something was considered good in the past, runs the assumption, there has to be a problem with it. But in spite of what her critics say, she did allow a degree of religious toleration and was nowhere near as severe or oppressive as her Roman Catholic rivals in France and Spain. The famous line usually attributed to her — "I will not make windows into men's souls" — could have been uttered by Sir Francis Bacon or even Sir Francis Walsingham describing the queen's philosophy, but it does epitomize her approach. Treason and threats to queen and country were dealt with severely, but having different opinions about the best way to worship Jesus Christ was often tolerated.

I've always relished another pronouncement attributed to her — oh, how I hope she really said it — made to the Earl of Oxford after he returned to England and to the royal court after seven years of self-imposed exile. The reason for his shame was that he'd once passed gas when bowing to his monarch. On his return, so many years later, Elizabeth welcomed him with, "My lord, I had forgot the fart"!

This birthday I feel old. I'm in my mid-sixties so that's hardly surprising, but what I mean is that I'm conscious of my age for the first time. In the past chronology seemed irrelevant since nothing seemed to change about what I could do physically. My parents were both gone by their mid-seventies, but I lead a healthier lifestyle than them, don't smoke, and listen to rather than ignore doctors. Still, genes are powerful indicators, and the cold embrace of the tomb seems far more immediate than ever before. I'm officially old too, because in a quite startling display of largesse, Toronto has given me just over a dollar's reduction on public transport.

In Britain, where I spent my first twenty-eight years, public transport in most places is largely free, outside of rush hour, when you hit sixty. Still, I'm grateful for small, very small, mercies. There's no escaping that I'm an old, white, straight male. Throw in "dead" and I've hit the jackpot, and hardly the most sought-after demographic in the age of the young and diverse. None of that bothers me very much, but losing friends to cancer or heart attacks at an exponential rate certainly does. It seems unstoppable right now. Beyond those I know and love are the ones I've never met. The deaths of famous people in sports, entertainment, or public life, people who represented stages in my childhood, youth, and happiness. Each death is like another brick in the wall of my being removed and discarded. Will I topple? It sometimes feels that way.

My health isn't bad all things considered, but I'm now on statins. My cholesterol was too high and my doctor, a saintly man who has been with our family for thirty-five years, will only recommend medication if he thinks it absolutely necessary. I struggled with the first types of statins I tried, suffering from long-term headaches and mild depression, but we finally found one that seems to work. I try to look on any medical experience as part of my clerical armoury — I've been there, so I know what it is and what it does. I had a case of this with atrial fibrillation, an abnormal heart rhythm that's not dangerous in itself but can be acutely uncomfortable and does increase the chances of a stroke. I'd had it for some time, but it got progressively worse, so my cardiologist discussed a surgical procedure called an ablation. I agreed, the surgery went well, and I felt no pain and hardly any discomfort in recovery. So, when someone came to see me to discuss how he was doing and mentioned that "afib" was making a dent in his life, I could describe what I'd had undergone. I told him that I have no medical expertise and that ablations aren't always successful, but that it did the trick for me. He underwent the procedure and now insists on thanking me almost every time he sees me.

I said in the introduction that I'd be honest, so here goes. I've just had to deal with a urology problem. Not one that is serious, but still very annoying and unpleasant. My doctor said I'd need a cystoscopy. I asked him what it was. He told me, crossing his legs as he did so. "You must be bloody joking!" I said. He explained that it wasn't as bad as it sounded. "That's not surprising," I said, "because it would be impossible for it to be as bad as it sounds!"

For those unfamiliar with the procedure, google it and weep. He was right, it wasn't as bad as it sounded, but I won't be taking it up as a hobby. I made the mistake of nervously chatting to the nurse when I entered the operating room. She was Australian, and I joked that England had "given your boys a good kicking" at a recent rugby game. "Yeah, they did," she said in a broad Melbourne twang. "But maybe it would have been better to have said that after rather than before the procedure." She was as gentle as a lamb. I think.

January 16

The Olympic athlete, gold-medal winner, and missionary Eric Liddell was born this day in 1902. I've a particular connection to him because in the early 1980s, I was hired as a researcher by the actor, playwright, and screenwriter Colin Welland, who wrote *Chariots of Fire*, for which he won an Academy Award. He took quite a chance with me because I was only recently out of university and had just started working as a journalist. Colin and I would become friends; he took me to his hometown of Newton-le-Willows in Lancashire, we attended rugby league games together, and I met any number of TV actors and even movie stars at his family parties. I was suitably impressed, and I think that rather amused him. He died in 2015 after living for some time with that cruel master, dementia. I still miss him. Colin had been a successful actor and writer since the 1960s but in 1982 won that Oscar for Best Original Screenplay for *Chariots of Fire*, in which Eric Liddell is one of the central characters.

The film itself was almost not made. The subject, two athletes who overcame prejudice and religious obstacles to win Olympic gold medals, was considered insufficiently popular. Those behind the idea disagreed, and its enormous international success proved them right.

One of the athletes was the Jewish sprinter Harold Abrahams, who faced antisemitic bigotry. The other was Eric Liddell who, as a devout Christian, refused to compete on a Sunday during the 1924 Olympic Games and was thus prevented from taking part in the qualifying rounds of the 100-metres, for which he was the favourite. He was moved to the 400, not his best distance, and won that convincingly instead.

Liddell was born in China to Scottish missionaries, members of the London Missionary Society, an interdenominational evangelical organization heavily influenced by Reformed and Congregational theology. The family returned to Scotland when Eric was a child, and he spent much of his youth in Edinburgh. He was a naturally gifted athlete, captained his school at cricket as well as rugby, while at the University of Edinburgh was regarded as the fastest runner in Scotland, and by 1922 was playing rugby for his country. Selection for the 1924 games was inevitable but — contrary to what *Chariots of Fire* presents — he discovered months before the games that the 100-metre heats were to take place on a Sunday. His refusal to compete made him a hero to some, Christian and non-Christian alike, but a villain to others. We can only imagine the response today, in the era of social media and instant and violent polarization.

Even within the British Olympic team there was a divided response. Liddell's coach was supportive, but others saw his behaviour as an example of religious extremism and a lack of patriotism only six years after the end of the First World War. What is less widely known is that Liddell's Sabbatarian views also prevented him from competing in the 4 × 400-metres relay, in which Britain won a bronze medal. Had he participated, the team would likely have won gold. He was, however, able to compete in and win the 400-metres, and earn a bronze medal in the 200-metres. Shortly before the final of the 400-metres, he was given a folded piece of paper by one of the team's masseurs (not, as the film shows, by a member of the U.S. team). It read, "In the old book it says: 'He that honours me I will honour.' Wishing you the best of success always." Liddell recognized the text from 1 Samuel and was deeply moved by the support.

He was a genuinely extraordinary athlete, achieving times that even today are remarkable. Yet his running style was unorthodox. Harold Abrahams once said, "People may shout their heads off about his appalling style. Well, let them. He gets there." What he wasn't, however, was some joyless puritan who defined his faith by what he refused to do. "We are all missionaries," he said. "Wherever we go we either bring people nearer to Christ or we repel them from Christ." And he did indeed bring people nearer to Christ. He was funny, humble, and approachable. His daughter once told me, "It always annoys me when people portray him as humourless and overly serious. That simply wasn't him."

As a national hero in Britain, he could have remained and enjoyed his popularity, but he returned to China in 1925, just a year after his Olympic triumph. He worked in the north, in Tianjin and then in Hengshui, Hebei province. It was a deprived area that had been devastated by China's civil war and then became a battleground for the invading Japanese. In 1941 the British government advised all nationals to leave due to Japanese expansion. Liddell was married and a father by then and sent his pregnant wife Florence and their children to Canada. But he remained, continuing to teach, work with local doctors, and also compete in local amateur races, mainly to entertain the community. He remained fast even without regular training and was asked if he ever missed the life he'd once had. "It's natural for a chap to think over all that sometimes, but I'm glad I'm at the work I'm engaged in now. A fellow's life counts for far more at this than the other."

By 1943 the Japanese occupied the surrounding area, and Liddell was one of those interned. Not all of the Westerners in the camp behaved nobly but he was renowned for sharing all supplies equally, organizing games, and refusing to give up his teaching and his Bible classes. Yet by 1944 he was beginning to feel unwell, lacking his usual energy and enthusiasm, and thought that he was suffering some sort of nervous breakdown. It was in fact a brain tumour, and a combination of lack of food, overwork, and poor conditions made survival impossible. He died on February 21, 1945. According to another missionary at the camp, his last words were "It's complete surrender," a reference to his submission to God. Theologian Langdon Gilkey was in the camp with Liddell and said, "He was overflowing with good humour and love for life, and with enthusiasm and charm. It is rare indeed that a person has the good fortune to meet a saint, but he came as close to it as anyone I have ever known."

He remains beloved in China, has inspired numerous people internationally, and Alan Wells, who won the 100-metre gold in the 1980 Olympics, dedicated the win to him. Perhaps the last word should go to Colin Welland, who made the great Christian athlete famous once again. "I'm an atheist, always have been," he said. "But if one man could change my mind it would be Eric Liddell. God bless him." By an odd coincidence, in one of the churches where I trained, I was approached one Sunday morning by a woman who said, "Hello, I'm Eric Liddell's daughter." I was stunned and not altogether convinced. But she was indeed his daughter, left behind in Canada with her mother when Eric returned to China as a missionary. She never saw him again.

January 20

Dumbing down, which has become a virtual art form, troubles me. Reality television, social media, instant gratification, the cult of emotionalism, and political narcissism have caused incalculable damage, and it's all rather dark and sombre. But I will not go gently into that dark night and won't go conservatively or angrily either. I see an increasing number of once-liberal people becoming reactionary as they age, blaming younger people for anything that annoys them, and that just won't do. My experience of those in their teens and twenties, largely through my four children or students whom I sometimes teach, is rejuvenating rather than depressing. Kids working two jobs so as to pay for college, having a genuine rather than ostentatious concern for the planet and for those around them, and being far more accepting and tolerant than were those of my generation. It's easy to mock their enthusiasms, but with some obvious exceptions, they have authentic empathy with the marginalized and persecuted. Complacency isn't some privilege we're suddenly awarded once our pension kicks in, and we should learn from the young rather than dismiss them. Be enlivened by the sometimes-stinging but still fresh winds of change; they make life much more enjoyable.

I do sometimes think of what I'll leave behind, but I'm sure that my books and journalism will soon be forgotten; with a handful of exceptions that fate applies to every writer. No, my legacy will be what I did for others. Every person I've tried to help, every meagre act of generosity, every act of forgiveness, every effort to try to do the right thing, to support those who are forgotten, my sacrifices, and my attempts to simply make things better. These are small contributions to the timeless and seamless world of kindness and goodness. The transformative aspect of the human condition is what lives on after us.

And children. I've tried my best as a father, failed on numerous occasions, sometimes miserably. But the children seem to have turned out rather well in spite of me, and what every parent should know is that the only thing that matters is to love unconditionally, which is the most difficult love of all. The doors of antiquity are now open wide, not to despair but to hope and faith. Is the world changing? Yes, thank God.

January 22

Synods are church gatherings of clergy where issues of doctrine and administration are discussed. We have them at various levels in the Anglican church, and while they can be heated and there can be disagreement, for the most they're friendly and some of the few occasions when clergy can meet as a full group. Unlike the wonderfully named Cadaver Synod in January, 897, at which Pope Formosous was given an ecclesiastical trial. He'd been dead for seven months so had to be exhumed and brought in less than good condition to a hearing conducted by Pope Stephen VI. The dead man was accused of perjury and also of having become pope illegally. He was found guilty and had his papacy declared null and void. There is no record of the judge asking, "And what do you have to say for yourself?"

January 27

I'm asked to write an article about J.R.R. Tolkien, the creator of *The Lord of the Rings* and *The Hobbit*. The reason is that I wrote a biography of the man some years ago and still receive letters from people who assume that I knew him or know something secret about him — Tolkien fans can be an "interesting" bunch. I once had someone approach me at the end of a church service saying he wanted to ask me a question. Of course, I replied. "He's not dead, is he? I know he's not." I inquired as to whom he meant. It was Tolkien. I said that he *was*, actually, and had been so since September 1973. "Oh, you're just like the bloody rest" said the disappointed zealot, before wandering off into the morning mist.

This commission is about Tolkien's religious faith and that pleases me, because Christianity was at the heart of the man's life and ripples of that emerge in his writing. Yet he could be somewhat enigmatic and inconsistent, even teasing, about the connection between faith and writing. While he described *The Lord of the Rings* as "a fundamentally religious and Catholic work," he also stated in an interview that "I cordially dislike allegory in all its manifestations, and always have done so since I grew old and wary enough to detect its presence." That was one of the reasons that he was so critical of C.S. Lewis's Narnia stories. But themes — yes, allegories — of creation and fall, sacrifice and sin, resurrection and redemption, darkness and light, and good and evil permeate his writing, and it is almost impossible to conceive of a Tolkien world detached from a Christian foundation. He once wrote to a friend: "I am a Christian, and whatever I write will come from that essential viewpoint."

He was three years old when his father died. His mother, a far from prosperous widow in Edwardian England, had become a Roman Catholic, and received generous support from local priests in Birmingham. She died when Tolkien was twelve, having given his guardianship to one of those priests, Father Francis Morgan. It was Morgan who pretty much raised the boy. From then on, there is no evidence that Tolkien ever really wavered in his faith, although the same cannot be said of his wife, Edith. She had been raised an Anglican, changing to Roman Catholicism largely because of Tolkien's insistence three years before they married in 1916. She later distanced herself from the Roman Catholic Church and resented her husband's taking their children to Mass. While the couple managed to reconcile their differences, Edith would never share her husband's dedication to Roman Catholicism, and it's unlikely that she was even a regular churchgoer.

While that may seem entirely unremarkable today, it must have been deeply painful to Tolkien. In one of his letters he wrote: "The only cure for sagging or fainting faith is Communion. Like the act of Faith, it must be continuous and grow by exercise. Seven times a week is more nourishing than seven times at intervals." And: "Out of the darkness of my life, so much frustrated, I put before you the one great thing to love on earth: The Blessed Sacrament." Tolkien's grandson, Simon, told of attending church with his grandfather in Bournemouth, after the liturgy had changed from Latin to English in the 1960s. Tolkien "obviously didn't agree with this and made all the responses very loudly in Latin while the rest of the congregation answered in English. I found the whole experience quite excruciating, but My Grandfather was oblivious. He simply had to do what he believed to be right."

Yet there's something timeless and even progressive about the man and his faith: his startlingly early awareness of environmental challenges and demand for responsible dominion over creation; his insistence on the importance of simplicity and warnings of the dangers of wealth and materialism; an acknowledgement of the temptations of power and a grasp of brokenness and inner beauty. It is those qualities, as opposed to formal religiosity, that have led to his enduring popularity. One of his earliest dedicated readership was the hippie movement of the 1960s: a subculture known for rejecting rather than embracing organized faith. And it could be argued that, for some — lovers of science-fiction, progressive-rock fans, New Age believers, for example — Tolkien has become an alternative to the very orthodox Christianity that he revered.

He was aware of this conundrum and often amazed at some of the letters that he received from devotees. But it is to his credit that this bemused rather than disturbed him: his faith informed his personality for the better and the brighter.

There is a revealing story that is worth the retelling. In 1938, when far too many people, Christians included, were still ambivalent about Hitler's Germany, a Berlin-based company considered producing a German translation of *The Hobbit*. Tolkien told his publisher that he considered Nazi race doctrines to be "wholly pernicious and unscientific." The German publisher eventually wrote to him, asking for a guarantee of his "Aryan descent." In his response, Tolkien dismissed the definition as absurd, and then explained that's he's not Jewish. "I regret that I appear to have no ancestors of that gifted people."

He was one of the good guys.

The good guys. Many years ago, I was watching a Western movie on television with our youngest son, and in between the bullets being fired and the arrows being shot, he suddenly turned to me and in perfect seven-year-old innocence asked, "Dad, who are the good guys?" It's a question we should regularly ask, of ourselves and about others. It's a coming-of-age thing, a vital admission that we too can behave badly, and from honest reappraisal comes a stronger and better person. Let truth unfold and allow the consequences to build and refine us. That's what good guys do.

January 31

My grandson is two years old. I won't name him or his parents because in this broken world there are people who hate and hurt others, and while I myself can take it — and have to do so most days on social media — I must protect my family. That reality, in fact, illustrates why new, pristine, gorgeous life is so important. Because there is too much darkness, too much pain, too much suffering and anger out there. Then along comes a tiny ray of light, extending and renewing hope and promise. In his cries and laughter, he is all of the world's sparkling possibilities personified.

Well-meaning friends have said that grandchildren are the reward for parenting. This suggests that parenting is some kind of torture. Sorry, I disagree. I loved, still love, being a father, and bless the fact that we have four children.

My mum was in Toronto on holiday from Britain when our third child was born. I always remember taking her to the airport and the woman checking her in asking if she'd had a nice time. "Yes," said Sheila Coren in her best East-End London accent. "I saw my grandson born." The Air Canada official replied, "Well, I'm going to make it a nice journey home too. I'm bumping you up to business class." It was the only time my mum ever flew business class. It was also the last time I saw her before the hellish blanket of dementia wrapped its filthy arms around her. She declined horribly quickly, fell into a coma, and then passed from us.

I can no longer tell my mum that I love her, but in the years I have left I can tell my grandson how much I love him and tell his parents how much I love them. Tell my other children, their partners, my wife, and all of the members of the cast that keep our little play going. Love isn't, as the Valentine's Day cards tell you, "never having to say you're sorry"; it's telling people how much they matter, how much they mean, and how much you need and want them. Birth and love, care and sacrifice, community and collective, empathy and apology, giving and knowing. Good news that sings words of incalculable beauty. I've no idea what my tiny grandson will become or what he'll do later in life, and I couldn't care less. If he's happy and makes others happy, the truth has won once again. And when I'm gone, and he remembers grandpa while looking at photos of the funny-looking bald man who wore a collar and wrote some columns, I simply want him to be able to say, "I loved him." That's all. This may seem very small and insignificant, but love is what transforms the world. I know that to be true, because I see it every single day.

February

February 2

A woman in her late seventies came to see me to discuss her son. He'd recently been released from prison for viewing obscene online images of children. Such things are no longer referred to as "child pornography" — a horribly flippant phrase — because pornography implies consent. It's one of the things you learn when working with people in prison and with the police. She didn't want to discuss too many details, but I knew from other offenders that his incarceration was likely the penalty for more than having looked at a single picture. Prison sentences are more often given as a punishment for distribution or sharing of these appalling things or viewing a large amount of such material. The actual manufacture of child abuse images is, of course, even more hideous and serious, but simply sending pictures can be classified as manufacture, even if the accused didn't actually take the photo.

The son had no interest in seeing me, but his mother was in an awful state. The man's release conditions demanded regular counselling, probation, being a specified distance from schools or wherever young people gathered, and a strong recommendation that he not use the internet (which is almost impossible to enforce and frequently ignored). He was also, she said, taking an antidepressant that helped to reduce his libido. Sometimes this does help, but the offender has to be willing to change and that's not always the case. But even when there's a desire to break the morbid and tragic cycle, there are instances where nothing works.

This poor woman cried, she screamed, she swore. All these responses are inevitable and far from unwelcome as part of the catharsis. I've seen them many times and if they help someone cope, then they work. I listened, which is often the best way to respond and usually what the person wants. Never pretend you have all or even any of the answers. We worked out a practical way of dealing with some of her feelings as well as how to approach her son when he seemed unreasonable, and we also worked on her not blaming herself for what had happened. It genuinely wasn't her fault, and she had to learn to value who she was.

She'd come to see me as a priest, so we discussed how she, as a Christian, should move forward. We can't believe in God, can't genuinely love God, I said, unless we believe in and love ourselves. That doesn't mean self-regard, pomposity, or pride, but coming to terms with the preciousness of the broken and the sparkle of the needy. We're flawed, we get it wrong, we can be difficult to like, but until we come to respect ourselves and see our reflection in the divine, we can never fully love others. That, and not some arcane philosophical puzzle, is the foundation of belief. She listened with an intensity I seldom see. Then we prayed. If you think this is perfunctory then you've never really prayed.

We continue to meet, to talk, and to pray. She thanks me a lot, which I'm supposed to say isn't what I want to hear but that's rubbish. It's not what the process is for but I'm no saint, and praise and thanks are as significant to me as criticism and condemnation. We can't expunge our human nature when we're ordained, and I worry about those who think they can or that they have. That notion of a priest being beyond flesh and blood and someone who can do no wrong has led to all sorts of problems, as we know too well.

On one occasion after she'd thanked me and said some lovely things, I thought that I needed to burst her bubble, so I asked her if she knew the definition of an Anglican priest. She said she didn't. I told her a story. There was an old-fashioned hairdresser in the middle of the city. One day, a Roman Catholic priest came in for a haircut. Afterwards, when he went to pay, the barber said, "No charge. I'm not Catholic, not religious, but I admire what you do. It's my gift." The priest thanked him, blessed him, and left. The next morning when the barber went to open the store, he found a bottle of Irish whiskey waiting for him. A month later a rabbi came in for a haircut. Afterwards he went to pay. "No charge, rabbi," said the barber. "I'm not Jewish, not religious, but admire your people so much. My little gift for you." The rabbi thanked him profusely. The next morning when the barber went to open the stop there was a large bag of freshly baked bagels waiting for him. Next month an Anglican priest came in. After the haircut he went to pay. "No, vicar," said the barber. "I'm not Anglican, not a Christian really, but I know the good work you do. Please, no charge." The priest thanked him from the bottom of his heart. The next morning when the barber went to open the shop, there was a long line of Anglican clergy at the door. That, I said, was the definition of an Anglican priest.

It was the first time I'd seen her laugh in three months.

February 3

Early on Sunday morning I take Tilly, our Parson Russell Terrier, out for a walk. I relish those early hours alone, drinking in the silence. I usually pray as I walk, and a special rhythm develops, stopped only when Tilly stops because she needs to do what dogs need to do. The earthy reality of a faith-filled life. She stops, arches her back, and does her thing. I bend down to scoop it up and then discover that there's a large hole in the bottom of the poop bag and my hands are covered. There's no bathroom around, of course, and I've a twenty-minute walk home with my hands covered in the stuff. The earthy reality of a faith-filled life no longer seems as appealing as it did when I left home.

February 4

An English bishop once told the General Synod of the Church of England that the term "woke" shouldn't be used negatively, as it is so often by conservatives who feel threatened by the social justice movement. The bishop was far from alone, with some leaders in her church and in mainline churches the Western world over advocating courses in "unconscious bias" training. Fair enough, I suppose, and the devaluation of language within political discourse has indeed become a scandal. Just as some on the Right routinely accuse opponents of being "woke" or Marxist, those on the hard Left throw the term "fascist" around with an offensive disregard for truth, let alone how they've distorted "Zionist" and perverted what was a word to describe a liberation movement for a persecuted people into a term of abuse.

But there's another issue here involving organized Christianity, and one that goes beyond semantics. It's the liberal, perhaps "woke," churches that are so often in worrying decline. There are exceptions of course, but generally speaking, growth is within more conservative churches, in Latin Mass Catholicism, *Book of Common Prayer* Anglicanism, and intelligent megachurch evangelicalism. I say this, by the way, as a social democrat, an old-style radical who believes in social justice and redistribution of wealth. Individual leaders with a particular charisma or appeal might make a difference and break the trend, but otherwise the pattern is fairly clear. It's usually the case that the more traditional the beliefs and worship, the greater their popular appeal. This isn't merely the result of older people clinging to what they've known; it's also the under-forties, often under-thirties and teens, who are searching for something that isn't a thin replica of what they see, hear, and learn in secular society. Sometimes these churches are quite socially conservative too, especially around issues of same-sex blessing and marriage, but that's not always the case, especially in North America. A fascinating scenario has developed where young Christians or seekers who have long held progressive views on gender, marriage, and even party politics feel the need for a more timeless theology and spirituality.

It is ironic that older Christian leaders have convinced themselves that younger people want "relevance" when what they actually mean is that they believe that next generation should be just like them. With the triumph of social media and twenty-four-hour news, it's virtually impossible to be contemporary, and teenagers and young parents know this all too well. They want an alternative to their daily lives, not a pale imitation of the commonplace, even the banal. Musically, give them Byrd or Bach rather than embarrassing versions of what the middle-aged think is popular, and for hermeneutics give them educated homilies centred on Biblical truth. I'm genuinely conflicted myself, being an orthodox Christian with traditional views on most aspects of theology who also believes in socialist economic principles, LGBTQ2S equality, and universal human rights and dignity. That's not to say that there isn't a great deal of pain and shame in the history of the church that we need to acknowledge which demands contrition and repair. I speak as someone whose family fled pogroms, often inspired by local priests. But that doesn't change the meaning and truth of authentic Christianity. Doesn't change the undeniable attraction of an orthodox faith delivered with sensitivity, empathy, and an informed understanding of the realities of this unforgiving and sometimes cruel age.

When I abandoned religious conservatism around twelve years ago, I was accused of having lost or diluted my faith. In fact, the opposite was the case. I changed not in spite of but because of my faith. As that faith deepened, it led me to different positions on various topics. My reformation was due to a commitment to Christian teaching rather than to political fashion or trendiness. C.S. Lewis once wrote, "Liberal Christianity can only supply an ineffectual echo to the massive chorus of agreed and admitted unbelief… Did you ever meet, or hear of, anyone who was converted from scepticism to a liberal or demythologised Christianity?" Mind you, the great Jack Lewis may well come with a trigger warning in some of our churches today. I wish I didn't have to write this, but I care passionately about the future of intelligent, progressive, devout Christianity, and I worry that we're losing battle after battle, not grasping that what seems appealing within the progressive bubble may be irrelevant outside of it. I was once told off by a priest for beginning my homilies with "In the name of the Father and the Son and the Holy Spirit," and criticized because my homilies were based on orthodox belief.

February 6

On a trip to Niagara Falls, I visit the Monastery of Mount Carmel. It's a Roman Catholic retreat centre where Anglicans often gather and where I spent my pre-ordination retreat. The Carmelites here have a particular devotion to Titus Brandsma, and so do I. He was born in February 1881, ordained a priest in 1905, and taught in numerous universities in the Netherlands. When the Germans invaded in 1940, he worked to oppose the Nazis, and in 1942 he personally delivered a letter from the Conference of Dutch Bishops to various editors of the country's Catholic newspapers ordering them not to print official Nazi material. He told each one, "We have reached our limit. We cannot serve them. It will be our duty to refuse Nazi propaganda definitely if we wish to remain Catholic newspapers. Even if they threaten us with severe penalties, suspension, or discontinuance of our newspapers, we cannot conform with their orders."

He visited fourteen editors before he was arrested. He was held at Scheveningen, Amersfoort, and Cleves, and then moved to Dachau concentration camp. He was murdered with a lethal injection on July 26, 1942, by a nurse of the Allgemeine SS in accordance with the medical extermination of prisoners. It is said that he gave the nurse his rosary and that when she told him that she didn't know how to pray, he replied that all she needed to say was "Pray for us sinners." The woman would eventually become a Christian and testified in Brandsma's canonization process.

His body was never found and was likely cremated. There are many such stories of Christian heroism and martyrdom during the Second World War, but they don't obscure the fact that churches and church leaders didn't do enough in the face of absolute evil. I'm often asked to speak on this topic, especially in regard to Pope Pius XII. Eugenio Pacelli had been elected to the papacy in March 1939 and remained Pope until 1958. The times demanded a man of strength and resolve, whereas Pacelli was a diplomat and a compromiser. Those attributes, rather than any extremes of personality or policy, characterized his personality and papacy. But because he led the Catholic Church during the Holocaust and the eventual Nazi occupation of his country, such anodyne skills were simply inadequate.

It's been genuinely difficult to gain a fair understanding of where he stood. Immediately after the war, Pius was regarded as a friend of the allies and a rescuer of Jewish people. That portrait changed dramatically in 1963 with Rolf Hochhuth's play *The Deputy*, in which the writer claimed that Rome not only ignored the suffering of the Jews but tacitly and sometimes explicitly supported the Nazis. In 1999 came the British author John Cornwell's *Hitler's Pope: The Secret History of Pius XII*, whose title suggests the book's arguments. Six years later there was a counterblast in *The Myth of Hitler's Pope: How Pope Pius XII Rescued Jews from the Nazis*. The author was David G. Dalin, who is not only Jewish but a rabbi. The controversy has continued, with shots fired from all sides in the Pius wars.

In 2019, Pope Francis ordered that from March 2020, previously secret documents concerning Pius and the Shoah should be released to academics, and he then made them available to the general public. What began to be discovered was that Pope Pius was neither as grim as his critics claim nor as noble as his defenders maintain. As a cardinal, he had drafted an encyclical condemning Nazi racism and had it read from every pulpit, and as Pope, he employed Vatican assets to ransom some Jewish families held by the Germans. There were also Roman Jews hidden in the papal palace of Castel Gandolfo; he did save individual Italian Jews and did work on behalf of Jewish people who had converted to Catholicism or were married to Catholics. He was definitely not a friend to National Socialism.

The problem is that he was not a significant enemy either. His considerable intelligence sources — some of them strongly anti-Nazi — had informed him of the extent and barbarity of the extermination of the Jews, but at no time did Pius explicitly condemn the Holocaust. He had, after all, been the Vatican's ambassador to Germany, and knew the beliefs of the Nazis. As for the often-made defence that any public condemnation would have been impossible or led to further suffering, the question has to be asked: Further suffering for whom? There were 1.5 million children murdered in the death camps. Also, it was during the Pius XII pontificate that the church issued the decree against Communism, declaring that any Catholic who became a Communist was an apostate and to be excommunicated. This was after the war but at the height of Stalinism. Had Pius learned a lesson, or was Communism viewed with far more distaste than Nazism?

February 8

I go to the hospital to visit a woman in her nineties. She has had dementia for some time and now has pneumonia. Her husband, who is also ninety, is in the same hospital, and he's dying of cancer. Her daughter has flown for more than five hours to be with her mum and has been by her side for some weeks. That daughter is gay and is in a relationship that's lasted for more than thirty years. But her mum has never accepted her sexuality and refers to her daughter's "gay friend" rather than her "partner." It's not been easy; the daughter tells me that her mother is deeply homophobic. But she's still here for her because love conquers all. I find it deeply moving, especially as that love involves forgiveness, which is precious and somewhat rare in this painfully unforgiving age.

I've just been brought into direct contact with the concept of forgiveness because of some of my media statements about the Nobel Prize–winning author Alice Munro. There had been stunning revelations about the Canadian icon. Her second husband had sexually abused her young daughter. Munro knew of it, failed to support her, and even after a brief separation returned to her daughter's abuser. People who were deeply shocked and hurt by her actions asked me to explain how they could forgive her.

I told one person who called that it's not for me as a priest or a commentator to tell anybody how to respond to this situation. I'm not part of the family, not an abuse survivor, and someone else's pain is not mine. But as a priest I do deal with similar issues on a regular basis and know that forgiveness is fundamental to our emotional health. "Darkness cannot drive out darkness; only light can do that," said Martin Luther King Jr. "Hate cannot drive out hate; only love can do that." Problem is, we often believe that that our own sense of righteousness and self-esteem is intrinsically linked to how condemning we are of the latest wrongdoer. On social media, "I shout therefore I am." Our response is less about the person accused, the sinner if you like, than it is about us. Are we made better, bigger, and bolder by our roars of disgust, or made smaller by participating in the pile-on?

I've dealt with numerous family breakdowns, divorces, and arguments, and in virtually every case the well-being of the injured party is improved if they're able to forgive. It is, if you like, a case of enlightened self-interest. I was in awe at this woman's sense and sensibility, but as a general rule it's restorative and life-giving to expunge the outrage. Justice is one thing, a desire for revenge quite another.

Then there's the issue of separating the person from the failing or the crime, and in this case the artist from the art. For example, I adore the music of Richard Wagner. Not only did he have obscene opinions about Jewish people himself, but he inspired Hitler. He died before the rise of Nazism but there's a direct link between him and National Socialist ideas. I can't pretend that this isn't a challenge, but I still listen to Wagner's music, cry at its magnitude and romance, and am enthralled by its grasp of what matters.

The same applies to many of my literary heroes. Some of their personal actions and even public beliefs sting me to the core, but their words still move me. Alice Munro failed her daughter and her family, and I'm sure that some people — and I'd think especially women and those who've experienced abuse — will now approach her work with a viscerally different attitude. That's not only understandable and reasonable but in some ways inevitable.

But this queen of the short story, who seemed able to understand the nuances of relationships in an almost unique manner, still has so much to say to us. Read her differently, read her hesitantly, even read her with tears and a torn heart, but please still read her. If we allow someone's behaviour, however base, to dominate our reaction, we allow brokenness to triumph. I hope and pray, and believe, that we're so much better than that.

February 10

People sometimes assume that the children of Christian parents must be sheltered and controlled, and while that can definitely be the case, my experience has more often been that they can be wonderful in their lack of pretence and their willingness to be direct. One such child approached me to ask a question.

"If I tell people what I gave up for Lent, does that mean it won't come true?"

"You mean like a wish when you blow out the candles on a birthday cake?" I replied.

"Yes, that's right."

I pause, and then say, "Almost certainly."

The answer pleases him, and I see the little fellow wander off to tell his dad what the priest has said. The dad, a friend, looks at me and waves his finger while laughing.

February 11

I'm re-reading Michael Ramsay's book *The Christian Priest Today.* He was Archbishop of Canterbury from 1961 until 1974, and the book was published in 1972. In spite of being more than fifty years old, it remains one of the best works of advice for a cleric. In it he writes: "You put yourself with God, empty perhaps, but hungry and thirsty for him; and if in sincerity you cannot say that you want God you can perhaps tell him that you want to want him; and if you cannot say even that perhaps you can say that you want to want to want him!" That may sound passive, but in my weaker moments I've prayed over those words again and again. We learn more spiritually during times of weakness than we do in times of strength.

February 12

A friend in Toronto has died. Her death had been expected, and I was privileged to see her two days ago and to anoint her with holy oil. She and her husband of fifty-five years didn't have any children, there was little immediate family, and their friends had almost all predeceased them. This happens a lot with older people, and the consequent loneliness is a terror. When I left the grieving husband mid-evening, I promised I'd call him and gave him my direct number in case of an emergency. I telephoned him the next day to see how he was. There were happy noises in the background. His church knew what had happened and in the space of a few hours had organized a schedule according to which groups of people, some of them teenagers, would visit with food and drink and throw miniature parties in honour of his wife. A full two weeks were covered and, as one of the leaders said to me, "By that time we'll all be good friends." They helped to take care of the "sadmin" (the endless paperwork after a death) and made sure that this man in need was never without someone to speak to. The pain would never pass, of course, and dealing with loss is a long-term process, but this immediate assistance was priceless.

February 13

I've just finishing co-pastoring a Lutheran church for a year. The Anglican Church of Canada is in full communion with the Evangelical Lutheran Church in Canada, so we often cooperate. The reason for this wasn't a merry one as we were amalgamating two churches — one Anglican and one Lutheran — to combine congregations and resources. The two separate churches simply didn't have the numbers to continue independently, and while their savings would have maintained them for two or three years, there was little if any hope of long-term continuation. I was there to shepherd the Anglican element, and while it was painful to close a church, the new one has an admirable minister and is doing well. It only requires three or four new relatively young families with children to keep a church alive, but we're not blind to the fact that our members are ageing and that we're not attracting enough young people to the Anglican church. But predictions of denominational death are ridiculous. There's growth in numerous churches and I see it all the time.

Just this week I met with a couple in their late thirties who want to become Anglican. They were raised Italian Catholic, love the heritage, and still believe in the Gospels, but she is divorced. Her first husband was abusive and an adulterer, but this wasn't deemed sufficient to justify an annulment. "I can't believe for a moment that Jesus could have seen that man beat me, could have seen him come home drunk and stinking of the perfume of the woman he's just slept with, and not tell me I had a right to leave him and remarry. If the church wants to say that, the church can do so. I won't abandon Jesus because of it." She and her husband are now committed worshippers in an Anglican church a few miles away. They asked me if I'd be willing to baptize any children they have. "If your priest agrees, just try and stop me."

February 14

It's Ash Wednesday, marking the beginning of Lent. Palms from last year's Palm Sunday are burned and their ashes are used to mark the heads of people as a sign of penitence. The priest makes the sign of a cross and says, "Remember that you are dust, and to dust you shall return." Not the most optimistic of liturgical statements, but it's appropriately sobering and a necessary reminder of mortality. Many churches apply the ashes at two services, morning and evening, and those who receive them in the morning either rub them off — I sometimes see them doing this as they leave the church — or choose to keep them all day. In the late afternoon at a grocery store, I bumped into someone I knew vaguely and there it was, the dark smudge on his forehead. "I'd no idea you were a Christian," I said. He looked confused. "The ashes on your head." He thought for a moment and then said, "My six-year-old threw a toy car at me. The bruise is fading but it's still there." He did, thank God, see the humour of it all.

I always leave the ashes on my head. There are so many ways to spread the word and Mahatma Gandhi, not a Christian and quite critical of those who follow Christ, spoke of the evangelism of the rose. "Don't talk about it," he said. "The rose doesn't have to propagate its perfume. It just gives it forth, and people are drawn to it. Live it, and people will come to see the source of your power."

February 15

Lent usually begins later than this but always runs until Holy Week, which is in late March or early April. Holy Week, when we celebrate Easter, is what is known as a "moveable feast," unlike Christmas, for example, so the date can change. It's determined through a calculation known as *computus*, the Latin for computation, and is celebrated on the first Sunday after the Paschal full moon. This represents an attempt to link Easter with the Passover, and the calculation is determined by people who are far more intelligent and important than a mere parish priest like me.

The period leading up to the beginning of Easter is a time for people to rethink and regroup, and as an Anglican priest I'm allowed to hear what is called "oracular confession," whereby a penitent privately outlines their sins, and we give them a formal absolution. This confession is extremely unusual, unlike in the Roman Catholic rite, where it's formally required but not always observed. We absolve the entire congregation every service, which critics think is an easy way out. I disagree. I see it as basic humanity. I've several friends who were Catholic priests and have become Anglican clergy or just left the priesthood altogether, and one of them told me, "We had confession every Saturday from 10:00 a.m. to midday. I'd sit there for two hours and listen to person after person tell me that they'd masturbated. It's what is known as a mortal sin in the Roman Church, you see, so if they go by the book they have to confess before they can receive communion. I tried to say to them, to imply really, that the real sins were hatred, lack of charity and lack of kindness, injustice, but I'm not at all sure it was what they wanted to be told."

He was faithful to not breaking the seal of the confessional but did tell me that one man had told him that he had had sex with a Protestant. He replied that the woman's religion wasn't the issue but rather that sex should be within marriage, with one's wife. "No, no, no," said the penitent. "Not a Protestant, a *prostitute*!" He received a surprisingly light penance.

What I usually hear when people come to speak to me privately are accounts of family breakdown, affairs, abuse, pain, and loss. I've some training in therapy but if the situation appears too serious, I always refer people to professionals who I like and trust. What I do have is the experience of thirty-seven years of marriage, raising four children, paying bills and a mortgage, and negotiating the tough challenges of family life. As much as I respect Roman Catholic clergy, I'm not sure that a celibate, single man can provide the empathy and understanding necessary to respond properly to all of these situations.

As we venture in these Lenten lands, walk these Paschal paths, we Christians are supposed to remember the forty days Jesus spent fasting in the desert. We do so in part by abstaining from something that gives us ease or pleasure and also paying special attention to the set readings for the season. One of those readings, mentioned in all four Gospels, is of Jesus in the Jerusalem Temple. "He found people selling cattle, sheep, and doves, and the money changers seated at their tables. Making a whip of cords, he drove all of them out of the temple. He also poured out the coins of the money changers and overturned their tables." This was a religious as well as monetary issue, but it reveals an intense opposition to the economic status quo of the time, which was not radically different from that of today.

And consider some other readings pertaining to money. "Again I tell you, it is easier for a camel to go through the eye of a needle than for someone who is rich to enter the kingdom of God" (Mark 10:25, Matthew 19:24, and Luke 18:25) and "For I was hungry and you gave me food, I was thirsty and you gave me something to drink, I was a stranger and you welcomed me, I was naked and you gave me clothing, I was sick and you took care of me" (Matthew 25:35). And in Matthew 19:21, when a rich young man asks what he must do to obtain eternal life, Jesus replies that he should sell everything and give the money to the poor.

Then there are situations where Jesus juxtaposes war and peace, and his words in the original *koine* Greek are far more militantly opposed to violence than they appear in the English translation. And remember his insistence in Matthew 5:9 that "Blessed are the peacemakers, for they will be called children of God."

This is powerful, relentless, compelling stuff, and I wish we could communicate it to the world more effectively. But when we do speak the Gospel clearly and without editing and compromise, we're told that Christians are overly credulous. Which is ironic, in that the secular world has seldom been as open to acceptance and to naive reverence as it is now. We are inundated with TV celebrities, young royals, conspiracy theorists, flimsy self-help gurus. So many people adore them, defend them, and attack their critics with the fierce absolutism of holy crusaders.

What we are witnessing is not so much a lack of belief as a change in what and whom we believe. I still believe in God. Not the God of neurotic theocracy, not the God of stale fundamentalism that has reduced the creator to a divine bureaucrat, ticking off boxes of behaviour to judge whether we get into paradise or not. Those boxes, by the way, usually involve issues like abortion and sexuality that Jesus never discussed or, when he did, demonstrated a glorious and revolutionary indifference to. No, something far more nuanced and even paradoxical than that was revealed by him: the God of losers, the God of what at first glance are wrecked causes. Because, as Freud once wrote, if we were all to get what we deserved, we'd all get a good whipping.

There are numerous arguments for the existence of God, most of them ultimately as pointless as arguments for the deity's non-existence, but there's another way to approach this. The most central teaching of Christianity is Jesus's commandment to love God with all of our strength, heart, and mind, and to love our neighbours, indeed all other people, as ourselves. Yet do we love ourselves, do we believe in ourselves? This is the age when self-harm and depression are grimly common, and personal doubt is ubiquitous. If we've fallen out with anyone, lost belief in a person, it's ourselves. If authentic Christianity is anything, it's the contrary of "virtue signalling," that contemporary putdown used so promiscuously by reactionaries the world over. True Christianity is far from virtue signalling; it is the announcement of failure and fault. Remember, during the first Easter those closest to Jesus were in despair. After the crucifixion, they cringed in hiding and cowardice, certain that following Jesus had been a colossal waste of time. They had failed in love, they detested themselves, they abandoned what they had seen and heard, and as a consequence during that dark hiatus, they also failed in belief.

As a cleric, I see most aspects of human nature on a daily basis. The pain of the human condition is sometimes difficult to witness, and I would never be so arrogant and crass as to offer religious platitudes to those stuck in mud-thick suffering. What I have discovered is that when people experiencing gruesome pain know the inner peace that comes from self-knowledge — yes, that is a form of love — they're more able and willing to forgive, accept, and believe others. I can question my behaviour, blush at past actions, know that I can be and do better, and want to lead an improved life, but if I *hate* myself, I'm of no use to anybody. More than that, I can never come to know God in the way that God desires. True religion, good religion, is an affair, a leap of romance, a reciprocal relationship. Love God "and" love your neighbour as yourself; these are not mutually exclusive but inseparable and codependent. The Christianity I embrace, the passion I embrace, rests on a belief in and a love for humanity as much as it does on a belief in and a love for God. I am part of that humanity, and when we remove the personal aspect, we slide from inclusion into judgment, and from joy into hatred. The great conversation of love and belief continues, and we're all welcome participants.

On a more prosaic note, twenty years ago, I decided to give up food for Lent, to endure a total fast, which sounds ridiculous and dangerous, and something I'm certainly not recommending. For forty-four days I drank a glass of V8 every day, swallowed a vitamin pill, but ate absolutely nothing. The result was interesting. I had extraordinarily clear and vivid dreams, a certain spiritual awakening, a loss of weight that didn't last very long, and horribly bad breath.

My wife is a very tolerant woman. I wouldn't do it again but there are serious, deeply thoughtful and intelligent religious people who fast on a regular basis.

February 16

Alexei Navalny has died in a remote and terrifying penal colony in the Arctic. He was incarcerated and almost certainly murdered for challenging Vladimir Putin. During his trial in 2021, Navalny quoted the Gospel of Matthew, "blessed are those who hunger and thirst for righteousness," and described how the words of Jesus inspired his politics and activism. Unlike Donald Trump, he was always reluctant to make his faith overtly public or political but said that being a follower of Christ meant that he had "fewer dilemmas" and that scripture provided him with a guide. He spoke often of how he thought Jesus would behave in various situations. This assertion wasn't akin to those of people who attach WWJD ("What would Jesus do?") bumper stickers to their cars but something far more profound. He insisted on living a Christ-like life in the most appalling conditions and retuning to Russia knowing that he would be arrested and likely killed.

Navalny wasn't always supported in his faith, either by allies or opponents. Many in the anti-Putin movement are strongly atheistic, and some of the most strident supporters of the Russian despot are active in the Russian Orthodox Church. Nor was he a lifelong believer but came to faith later in life, as are a number of people, some quite prominent, who look for a spiritual and philosophical underpinning to their objection to oppression and tyranny.

This glaring difference, between those who try to twist the Prince of Peace into a reactionary warlord and those who see him as the great rebel he truly was, has always been there, of course. St. Francis of Assisi in the early 1200s on the one hand, medieval Popes with lavish palaces on the other. Anglican Bishops investing in the slave trade in the eighteenth century, and the abolitionist movement led by evangelical ministers and politicians. Church leaders in Nazi Germany remaining silent or saying little, and heroes such as Sophie Scholl giving their lives to oppose Hitler. The latter was beheaded for her Christian witness. She was only twenty-one years old.

February 19

The Polish writer Isaac Deutscher, renowned for his biographies of Trotsky and Stalin, was raised in a strictly orthodox Jewish family. He was praised as a child for his study and understanding of the Torah and the Talmud and expected to be a great rabbi. By the time he was a teenager, he was losing his faith and decided to give God one final test. He ate non-kosher food on Yom Kippur at the grave of a local holy man. When nothing happened, he said, "I became an atheist." I admire Deutscher's books, but his theology is wafer thin. God doesn't do banal, doesn't do instant answers. I sometimes wish he did, but then he wouldn't be God. We're his creatures, not his slaves or automatons.

I remember when our eldest child went to high school on his own for the first time. He was the right age, it would have been too smothering to hold him back, but we were nervous. I was waiting close to the front door at 4:00 p.m., even though he wouldn't be back for at least another thirty minutes. Then he appeared, gave a teenage grunt, and went up to his room. We had to let him go but we were so glad when he came home. God wants us back but has to let us go first. It's not about the type of food we eat or where we eat it. Isaac Deutscher should have known better.

February 23

Debbie comes to see me on a regular basis for fifty dollar shopping cards. We chat. "My doctor retired, and the new one won't see me very often," she says. "I don't blame him though, because he's overwhelmed with people." She's on various meds, can't afford all of them, so is selective in what she takes. That's not uncommon, and the notion that those on low income receive all the support they need is pure fantasy. "It used to be easier but now they're very strict. There's one drug they have me on, but it has some bad side effects. They've said I have to give it three months before they'll pay for an alternative." She takes a deep sip from a cup of strong tea. "I think I'll just stop taking it." I tell her that could be dangerous, but she just shakes her head. "If I die, I die. Not sure I really care anymore. I'm so damned tired of making phone call after phone call and nobody seeming to care."

In the afternoon I check in the local hospital reception to see if anybody would like to speak to a priest. A friend who works as an ICU nurse sneaks up and grabs me round the neck. We sit down at the hospital café, and I ask him how things are going. "Look, it's never been easy, but we now feel like we're almost an enemy of the administrators, the politicians, the government. I'm a realist. There were shortages under every government, but then it was as if we were in it together, on the same side. Not now."

The workload is worse than ever, and that's especially true in emergency rooms, where I spend a lot of time. Friday and Saturday nights have always been busy, but the volume of people on weekdays has increased extraordinarily. The reason is that people can't find family doctors anymore and have no option but to go to emergency wards for clearly non-emergency cases. "It's always been an issue," says the nurse, "but never like this. These people don't have doctors, and we don't have the time and resources." I ask him if he thinks anybody has ever died because they couldn't receive treatment quickly enough due to the numbers. "Of course, of course," he says without looking up.

February 26

The past few weeks haven't been kind. Within the space of twenty-four hours, two of my friends died, both with a suddenness that chilled me.

One was sixty-nine years old but robust, healthy, and always full of enthusiasm and determination. I'm so grateful that I visited Britain last December and saw him twice. One of those occasions was a long, exquisite lunch in a Turkish restaurant. That will be my invincible memory, but I am still shaken to the core by his death.

The other was a mere thirty-three. Painfully and unfairly young. I remember her as a baby; she knew my two daughters and was the same age as one of them. I also gave her a job on a television station where I once hosted a show, not because of who she was but because she was so funny, clever, kind, and mischievous. Oh, her poor parents, her poor friends and family.

I grieve with people all the time, hold them, hear them, try to heal them. I've also been at more hospital beds with the dying than I can remember, watching death's shadow emerge ever stronger and darker. It's always difficult but, all clichés aside, also a privilege. I'm trusted, people depend on me, and while I often feel totally inadequate, I know that the situation is not about me at all. All I can be is a conduit. Pull back the curtain and reveal Jesus. That's all.

But what when death is closer to home, more personal and intimate, more severe and cutting? I always recommend that people read *A Grief Observed* by C.S. Lewis: "No one ever told me that grief felt so like fear. I am not afraid, but the sensation is like being afraid. The same fluttering in the stomach, the same restlessness, the yawning. I keep on swallowing." So, I re-read it this week and, as always with Jack Lewis, found new answers and new truths. I prayed in a different way and asked for different strength. It helps, of course it helps. Prayer is central in all that we do, but at times of agony it matters more than ever. I genuinely believe that this is only the land of shadows, and real life hasn't begun yet, but can I rationalize pain and loss, especially when it's my own pain and loss? Frankly, not completely.

What I can and do say, and what I've reminded myself a dozen times in the past few days, is that Jesus has been there before us, suffered before us, and — vital this — suffered for us. In a divine leap of solidarity, he felt what we now feel. God became flesh, became a vulnerable, defenceless baby, a baby born to a poor family living in an occupied country, and having to run from tyranny and violence. As a grown man he knew his fate, knew that the cruellest execution of all awaited him, but embraced that agony out of pure, perfect love. Whatever we suffer, no matter how much we weep, God empathizes because God knows and understands. Because God became one of us.

One of my two friends who died was a Christian, and a priest and a bishop. That makes the context different and because of it I can be more direct in my approach to others and with myself. He was also, while not old, at least someone who had led a full life. The other was a young woman and Jewish rather than Christian. Not orthodox but certainly proud of her religion, as are her parents and family. She was also so jarringly young, with so much of her life still to live. That break in the natural order, the smashing of what ought to be, and the destruction of potential, leaves a wound that may never fully heal. I can pray and reflect privately about her in the same way but wouldn't dream of offering explicitly Christian answers to people of a different faith, especially at such a time and in the case of such tragedy. No, my approach at times like this, and it's certainly not the first time that dear friends who aren't Christian have died, is simply to be present.

March

March 5

We're approaching Easter, the historical geopolitics of which are complex. King Herod had ruled Israel for many years but died in 4 BCE. He was known as "The Great" (distinguishing him from other kings with the same name) and was a major player in the region, perhaps Rome's most significant client monarch. His kingdom was divided into three, one part of which, Judea, the Romans soon made a province under their direct rule. Galilee was given to Herod Antipas, King Herod's son, meaning that Jesus wasn't raised under Roman governance. There were lots of Greeks in Galilee, and lots of bandits too. It was multicultural and wild, and Jesus would have certainly known all sorts of people. The majority of Jews lived not only outside Galilee but outside the entire region. The diaspora has existed for a very long time.

As for Easter itself, there's no sacrifice, no resurrection, no salvation without the crucifixion. The Last Supper was the meal Jesus ate with his disciples before his execution during which he shared the bread and the wine "in remembrance of me." What Jesus's words mean — symbolically or literally — is still debated among Christians, but it was certainly a commandment. As was his plea that we love one another. The Latin for commandment is *mandatum*, from which we get the name Maundy Thursday. The synoptic Gospels (Matthew, Mark, and Luke) present the Last Supper as a Passover Seder, although it differs in some respects from the first-century norm. In that Mark and Matthew were Jewish, and Luke either a Hellenized Jew or a Greek who knew the Jewish world intimately, this presentation must have been intentional.

Shortly after the Last Supper, Jesus was arrested and then came the trial. Where it took place is still uncertain. The traditional view holds to Jerusalem's Antonia Fortress, built by Herod to honour his patron, Mark Antony. By the time of Jesus, a large part of the Roman garrison was stationed there. Luke says that when Pontius Pilate discovered that Jesus was a Galilean, he sent him to Herod and that Herod returned him to an unwilling Pilate. The Gospels aren't clear on the geography; it was later pilgrims who established the route of the Via Dolorosa, the stations of the cross. It's considered largely accurate but the starting point, the trial, will never be precisely known. In terms of the date, we know from non-Biblical sources that Jesus was crucified by Pilate during the reign of Tiberius, which provides a window of less than a decade.

The trial was conducted early in the morning before most people were awake. Pilate was a man promoted above his abilities, and he clearly didn't want to be involved in what he considered an esoteric Jewish squabble. Philo, a Jewish scholar and contemporary, condemns him as corrupt and cruel. He was certainly out his depth and largely unconcerned about what Jews, and Jesus, meant by messiahs and Christs. These were religious terms unusual to the Romans and considered absurdly rustic. When the Jewish leadership claimed that Jesus proposed himself as a rival king to Caesar, however, that was clearly treasonous and the Etruscan-invented crucifixion, a judicial murder for slaves but never Roman citizens, could be applied to him as a consequence.

When the verdict was announced, the crowd cheered. But does that really show the faithlessness of the mob? We're speaking of relatively small numbers and Jesus's opponents still had sufficient influence to sway a few hundred. Then there were the actual followers of Barabbas, the alternative candidate offered by Pilate for freedom. Contrary to what we're told, he was more likely a rebel leader than a criminal, and his advocates would have been organized and violent.

Crucifixion, a truly horrible way to die because it could take a long time, was public and exposed, and the dying victim would struggle to breathe and was often bitten by wild animals aroused by the smell of blood. Seneca wrote, "You must never mention crucifixion in polite company."

Then the resurrection. If you can believe this, the rest is easy.

The first Gospel, Mark's, was likely written between 64 and 72 of the common era, a mere thirty years after the events described in it. Numerous people would have been alive who'd witnessed them firsthand, so the author would have been dismissed as a lunatic or liar if they'd disagreed with his account. Many people who saw Jesus killed would go on to devote their lives to his cause, knowing what their own fate would be. People die for the wrong reasons, but never knowingly so. They believe and, in this case, they believed because of what they saw. There are differences of emphasis in the Gospels but no genuine contradictions. Within a little over three hundred years, more than thirty million people, perhaps the majority of those living in the Roman empire, believed as well.

The man who was released in place of Jesus, Barabbas, isn't mentioned in the Gospels after his release. It's likely that the Romans set him free because failure to do so would have caused a riot. As for Pilate, while he's mentioned in the creeds and is one of the most famous Romans in history, he was actually a minor figure. Little is known of his earlier career, but he ruled Judea under Tiberius for ten years from 26 or 27 CE. Josephus records that Pilate was removed after he heavy-handedly suppressed a Samaritan revolt. Rome wanted taxes, not expensive conflict. Tiberias died before Pilate reached Rome and there's no reliable record of the man after that.

March 7

Christian believers today come from all over the world and while there are problems of declining congregations in North America and western Europe, that's not an issue in Asia and Africa. The church in Ethiopia, for example, is extremely strong, and that country was Christian long before most of Europe. The Ethiopian church is Eastern Orthodox, and many Orthodox believers follow a different calendar from the Western one and celebrate Easter a little later. I discussed this with a young man from Ethiopia who I visit — he'd seen me on television once and emailed me to ask if we could meet occasionally to discuss the Bible. He's brilliant and bright but his accent is still quite pronounced, which has made it difficult for him to find work. We came to the end of our meeting today, said a little prayer together, and he buttoned up his coat so as to face the cold weather.

Suddenly he said, "I don't want to live." I was shocked, as this seemed to come from nowhere. I asked him why he felt this way, insisted that he would find a job eventually, and asked if he would like me to cancel my next meeting so that we could spend more time talking. Could I call his family, or even drive him to the hospital? I said that he must know that life is worth living and that there were so many things that gave him joy and happiness. I suppose I came on a bit strong, but I was genuinely worried about him. He stared at me, then in his forceful accent said, "What you talk about? I said I don't want to leave. Are you deaf! I don't want to leave; it's bloody raining out there!"

I drove him home.

March 9

As a child, Easter meant relatively little to me. It was chocolate eggs, films about Jesus on television, and something vague about a magical rabbit. All rather confusing. The confectionery and the bunny eventually became irrelevant, but the movies must have left an impact, because I became a Christian in my mid-twenties. But even now I'm deeply aware of the moral defect of antisemitism that has never died and is once again becoming grimly fashionable. That's especially poignant at Easter, which always comes with a certain ache for me. We remember the great commandment to love one another and take shelter from an increasingly hysterical and unforgiving world under the divine promises of Christ personified in the resurrection. Yet it's also the time when we read of "the Jews" as those who were responsible for condemning and killing Jesus. The phrase "the Jews," *hoi Ioudaoi* in the original Greek, is used more than sixty times in John's Gospel, and more than two dozen of those are painfully accusing. It's difficult to hear of Pontius Pilate saying to "the Jews," "Here is your king," and them replying, "Away with him! Crucify him!"

John's is the most troubling of the four Gospels in this regard but Matthew's Gospel, considered the most Jewish of the canon, has, "When Pilate saw that he was not succeeding at all, but that a riot was breaking out instead, he took water and washed his hands in the sight of the crowd, saying, 'I am innocent of this man's blood. Look to it yourselves.' And the whole people said in reply, 'His blood be upon us and upon our children.'" The reference is almost certainly to the destruction of Jerusalem in 70 CE but, misunderstood and exploited, those lines have caused incalculable harm. I still cringe a little when I listen to some of these texts, even though they're usually read by kind and loving members of my church who would be appalled if they thought they were perpetuating anything racist and damaging.

Words may be merely words, but their historical consequences are undeniable. Massacres of Jews often took place during Easter, not only in medieval Europe but in more recent times. Perhaps the most infamous, but certainly not unique, was the Kishinev pogrom in 1903, in what is now Moldova but was then part of the Russian empire. Mobs of Christians leaving church during Holy Week rioted for two days, murdering forty-nine Jews, seriously injuring a further ninety-two, and committing numerous acts of rape and violence. The horror gave impetus to the emerging Zionist movement and also led to a mass exodus of Jews from Russia and eastern Europe. My father's grandparents were among them.

The post-Holocaust church is radically different, of course; there's been a conscious effort within most Christian denominations to grasp the Jewishness of the narrative, and theologians have worked diligently to explain what is actually going on. Most of the people involved in this story of internal Jewish politics were Jewish, but by the end of the first century, there was direct competition between church and synagogue. The early church was overwhelmingly Jewish, but the expectation that all of Israel would follow Jesus simply hadn't materialized. This wasn't "antisemitism" as we'd understand it today, but more the frustration of believers that their Jewish brothers and sisters hadn't accepted Jesus as the promised Messiah. Part of the Christian attempt to rebuild relationships with the Jewishness of their faith has led to the phenomenon of Christian seders, particularly popular in certain evangelical circles. The theory is admirable, the planning and effort often impressive, but there's a danger on trying just a little too hard. Sometimes the details are wrong, it's unusual for Jewish people to be present, and it can be seen as cultural appropriation.

Back in 2010 I attended what is surely the most famous Passion Play in the world, held every ten years in Oberammergau, Bavaria, to depict the finals days of Jesus. The subject, the region, and the context are all tragically soaked in European antisemitism; historically, Easter could be a terrifying time for Jewish people. But this is the new Germany and the new church. What I witnessed on that cold night, with a thunderstorm above the exposed stage, was the sublime transformation of the Jew as Christ-killer to the Jew as Christ. Indeed, one of the reasons that the play is so long is that the contemporary script goes to such pains to emphasize the story's Jewish roots. The Temple merchants whom Jesus whips are hardly mentioned, Jesus Himself is constantly described as a rabbi, the Sanhedrin argue noisily over whether they should accept this new Messiah, and the menorahs are large, numerous, and unavoidable. Cynicism is easy but, in all honesty, I began to weep, especially when the German actor playing Jesus recited the first line of the *Shema* — "Hear, O Israel, the Lord our God, the Lord is One." After all, this was taking place in Germany, where in living memory so many Jews were slaughtered.

Recently a fellow priest asked me for some advice related to this issue. Members of his congregation, none of them of Jewish heritage, had asked him if the scriptural passages that were read during Holy Week could be changed so that "the authorities" could replace "the Jews." The priest in question asked me because of my own background, and I was touched by his and his congregation's sensitivity. I told him that while a few words of explanation in his homily or in a private conversation might be helpful, scripture was far too important to edit, and that education and understanding were always preferable to censorship and political tampering.

March 13

At its best, the church organizes goodness and directs it into places where it's most needed. That's not always the image that those outside of the church see and believe in, and when the media mentions Christianity, there's usually a scandal or an outrage involved. This week there's been another attempt in the U.S. to display the Ten Commandments in a public place, and that's produced an anti-Christian backlash. The first amendment to the U.S. Constitution states that "Congress shall make no law respecting an establishment of religion, or prohibiting the free exercise thereof," so these things usually fail, and then the instigators can declare themselves martyrs. The commandments given to Moses forbid adultery of course, yet the political hero of those who insist on pushing this agenda is Donald Trump, who is a repeat offender and has shown no contrition, not to mention his full bag of other sins and failings. Then there's the commandment not to murder, when support for placing these posters comes from some of the most zealous opponents of gun control in North America. The same people who, after every gun massacre, tell anyone who'll listen that they're praying to God for the victims. If that's not taking the Lord's name in vain — another commandment — I don't know what is.

But the issue runs deeper than mere hypocrisy. The Ten Commandments are vital to Christian thought as well as to the other monotheistic faiths, but the most important teaching of Christ is that we love one another. Perhaps we should campaign to have the Beatitudes on display in schools, telling us that the poor in spirit, the meek, the merciful, the peacemakers, the pure in heart, and those who are insulted and persecuted for the sake of righteousness are all blessed. But perish the thought, because those teachings delivered by Jesus during the Sermon on the Mount sound so radical.

At any rate, we don't need any of this; we need witness and action. Christianity is best represented by people living as followers of Jesus, helping those in need and in pain, evincing goodness and kindness, and sacrificing for the sake of others. In political terms that could be by improving public education, giving women reproductive choice and heavily subsidized daycare, fighting poverty, and spending money on housing and health rather than on tanks and torpedoes. It is least represented by loud, aggressive fundamentalists drowning in legalism and paranoia who somehow think that a few lines on a classroom wall will solve all of our problems. Sometimes I wonder if they even believe that themselves.

March 14

I bump into a Catholic priest at the hospital, where we're both visiting patients. He's a good and hard-working man, and we have a few friends in common. I see he has a book in his hand and ask what it is. "It's the new biography of Mother Teresa," he says. "I've a particular devotion to her." I smile and wish him a good day.

My first job in journalism was at *The New Statesman* magazine in Britain in the early 1980s. I was new and shiny and one of the first people I met was a man who was not new but shone in an entirely different way. Christopher Hitchens was as generous as he was gifted, though he didn't suffer fools or frauds. One of the most famous of the latter, in his opinion, was Mother Teresa, born in Albania as Anjezë Gonxhe Bojaxhiu, someone whom to many embodied the best qualities of Christianity. Hitchens disagreed, wrote a book about her called *The Missionary Position*, and insisted that she was a force for evil rather than good.

Hitchens's argument was that Mother Teresa provided substandard medical care, took money from dictators and criminals and often cozied up to them, pushed her faith on the vulnerable and sick, and encouraged Western Catholic journalists to portray her as divine. There are many unanswered questions about the level of aid the poor of Calcutta actually received because of her, and it is true that Mother Teresa was funded by brutes such as Jean-Claude Duvalier of Haiti, who stole a fortune from his own people while they lived in poverty. In fact, not only did she take the man's cash, but she also lionized him as a great leader. She also praised the repugnant Albanian despot Enver Hoxha and laid flowers at his grave and welcomed donations from British publisher and criminal Robert Maxwell.

A particularly disturbing case is that of the antipornography zealot and businessman Charles Keating. He gave millions of dollars to Teresa and offered her the use of his private jet when she visited the United States. Although he was sent to prison for more than four years for fraud and thousands of people were hurt by what he did, Teresa refused to refund any of the money he had donated.

"I think it is very beautiful for the poor to accept their lot, to share it with the passion of Christ," she said. "I think the world is being much helped by the suffering of the poor people." That is surely not how the poor themselves feel as they watch their babies die in their arms. There are many Christian groups performing outstanding work in India and elsewhere who do not adopt Teresa's dubious ways, and do not have or want the public relations machine that she enjoyed.

March 16

Of course, people and things can change. I read today of someone I knew many years ago when I was a teenager in east London. He led a fascist group in the 1970s, edited a racist magazine, and was eventually sent to prison for eight months. It was while incarcerated, often in solitary confinement, that he began to read Christian authors, began to think and to pray; he eventually became a Christian, and has devoted his life to faith and scholarship. He left the world of hate for the world of love.

In a different way this ability to change applies to me as well and is something I spoke about this week to a group of LGBTQ2S Christians at a public meeting. My change of belief seems like ancient history but only took place a little over a decade ago. When that change first happened, I'd never be sure what reception I'd receive from gay audiences, but I needn't have worried. Now, after ten years of contrition, work, apology, and activism, it would take a committed person to still hold a grudge against me.

On this evening, I gave the Biblical arguments for equal marriage and full Christian acceptance and equality of gay people. The Bible hardly mentions homosexuality, which is of course a term not coined until the late nineteenth century. The so-called gotcha verses from the Old Testament are specific to ancient customs and are often misunderstood. The Sodom story, for example, wasn't interpreted as referring to homosexuality until the eleventh century. Lot — the hero of the text — offers his virgin daughters to the mob in place of his guests, so it can't exactly be used as a compelling morality tale! Ezekiel in the Hebrew Scriptures says, "This was the guilt of your sister Sodom: she and her daughters had pride, excess of food, and prosperous ease, but did not aid the poor and needy. They were haughty, and did abominable things before me" (Ezekiel 16:49–50).

The Old Testament never speaks of lesbianism, and its mentions of sex are more about procreation and the preservation of the tribe than personal morality and romance. It also has some rather disturbing things to say about slavery in Genesis and in Paul's letter to the Ephesians, about ethnic cleansing in Deuteronomy, and even about killing children in First Samuel. So, a precise guide to modern manners it's certainly not. Jesus doesn't mention the issue, and St. Paul's comments, mainly in his letters to the Romans, are more about men using young male prostitutes in pagan initiation rites than about loving, consensual same-sex relationships.

There is one possible allusion to homosexuality in the New Testament when Jesus is approached by a centurion whose beloved male servant is dying. Will Jesus cure him? Of course, and Jesus then praises the Roman for his faith. The Greek word used to describe the relationship between the Roman and his "beloved" servant indicates something far deeper than mere platonic affection. Then there's the love of David and Jonathan, Jesus refusing to judge, and the beauty of grace and justice that informs the Gospels.

As I was explaining all this, a young man at the back stood up and said, "Yes, that's good, and I agree but I want to know why you, why you changed. I'm so glad you did, I read you all the time, but I need to know why. I need to know." There were some nods of agreement, then silence. This wasn't criticism and certainly not hostility but genuine interest, even affection. Then he began to choke up. Then he started to cry. "I'm sorry, I said I wouldn't do this, I'm sorry," he said. I apologized if I'd said or written anything in the past that had hurt him. "No, not really," he said. "I only got to know you after you'd changed." A pause. "It's just that this all makes me so hopeful, so happy. Yet I'm crying. Stupid, just stupid."

It wasn't though, and as I finished my talk there were tears in my eyes too.

March 18

I begin each day with Morning Prayer, following the Anglican office of prayers, psalms, and readings. In many ways it's my favourite time of day and the main reason I set the alarm to 5:00 a.m. That exquisitely lonely hour, usually still dark, has always felt special to me, and I'm sure it does to many people. I make my coffee, sit in my study, and open the day. Yes, I open the day. I used to use the Canadian version of morning prayer but now use three separate books: the *Book of Alternative Services* (BAS), the Bible, and something called *McCausland's Order of Divine Service*. The first contains the order and structure of morning prayer, as it does most of the other elements of Anglican worship. The second has, obviously, the various readings set for that day. The third lists what is to be read for Morning Prayer as well as the other daily services. That's a lot of turning from one book to another. Morning Prayer is easier with the *Book of Common Prayer* (BCP), but I've been introduced to the Church of England's prayer online. The structure is slightly different from the Canadian version and the readings aren't always the same, but I'm confident that God isn't too fussed. It's so convenient having it on a screen on my phone, and there's audio as well so I can hear the psalms sung properly and beautifully, and sometimes join in. We had friends staying recently and over breakfast one of them said to me, "I think you were having a nightmare this morning. I could you hear making noises, like a troubled chant." A troubled chant, the unknown psalm.

Perfunctory prayer, praying because you have to or for the sake of it, isn't prayer as it should be. It removes the nourishment of this privileged conversation with God, reduces a sublime dialogue to sheer banality. It's rather like a handshake or a casual "How are you?" — they once signified visceral feelings but now mean hardly anything at all. The crucial point about authentic prayer is its raw honesty. It should open us up, revealing intimacy and vulnerability, leading us to question our actions and filter our emotions and feelings through a prism of goodness and kindness. Prayer is difficult and challenging and is supposed to change us rather than change

God. If we pray so as to be seen, pray to be noticed, we are not only getting it wrong but positively shaming the purpose of the practice. Jesus is especially hard on those who pray in public so that onlookers will have a higher regard for them.

I'm not accusing politicians of this; those I know personally who are people of deep faith are among the least likely to make a loud noise about public prayer. The great paradox of Christianity is that in defeat is victory, and that's a problem for any ambitious politician. Martin Luther King, a man who dedicated his life to social and political change, and was certainly not afraid to pray in public, said: "Although prayer is native to man, there is the danger that he will misuse it. Although it is a natural outpouring of his spirit, there is the danger that he will use it in an unnatural way."

March 19

Speaking of the *Book of Common Prayer*, I've just led a morning Eucharistic using it. At the end, a student from the local university approached me and said, "Hey, Rev, cool language. Never heard that before in church. I may even come again." I was about to explain the origins of the text and its evolution when, entirely wisely, the young man stuck his earbuds in, turned on his music, and waved goodbye. "I'll be back," he shouted as he left. I doubt he was listening to William Byrd or Thomas Tallis, but he has been back.

That's not as rare as you might think. Contrary to what we've been told for decades about younger generations wanting the contemporary and the modern, my experience — as both a father and a priest — is that the kids are too savvy for that. They can distinguish between language directly influenced by Shakespeare and language written by a committee based on diversity, sensitivity, and inclusion. It's the same in the Roman Catholic Church; arguably even more so. The Latin Mass, or even the Mass in the vernacular in an older form, is surprisingly popular among younger people longing for something permanent. I admire Pope Francis in many ways, but his attacks on — even persecution of — the Latin Mass are unwise, downright cruel, and extraordinarily counterproductive.

The BCP, the *Book of Common Prayer*, contains sublime language: "Land of the living," "A tower of strength," "At death's door," "Peace in our time," "At their wits' end," "Softer than butter," "From ashes to ashes, dust to dust," "To have and to hold," "In sickness and in health," "Till death us do part," and so on. The book we use now dates from 1662, but that's a little misleading. Its origins are earlier, and there have been edits since. The first prayer book was published in 1549, shortly after Henry VIII's death. It's wrongly assumed that the old swine founded the Church of England but in many ways, he held it back. His break was purely with Rome, and that attitude wasn't uncommon among otherwise traditional Catholics in sixteenth-century Europe. When he was succeeded by his genuinely Protestant son Edward VI, authentic reforms could take place. The original BCP was the first prayer book to contain all the weekday and Sunday services in English.

Another, more Protestant version was published in 1552. When Edward VI died the following year and his Catholic half-sister Mary came to the throne, it was the temporary end of the book and permanent end of the man most responsible for it. In 1556 Thomas Cranmer, by then sixty-six years old and unwell, was imprisoned, humiliated, and then burnt to death. He had been an important advocate for Henry VIII's divorce from Mary's mother, Catherine of Aragon, so this was personal. He was also the mind, soul, and skill behind much of the BCP. Elizabeth I reintroduced the book in 1559, including some edits to satisfy the conservatives. The Anglican church may seem relatively Catholic today, but Cranmer was an authentic Protestant, heavily influenced by the Swiss reformer Ulrich Zwingli.

When the Parliamentarians won the Civil War, they abolished the BCP. We sometimes forget how persecuted the Church of England was under the Puritans. So when Charles II was restored to the throne, the book was returned, and its 1662 version is largely what we have today, in 50 countries and 150 languages. It's arguably more responsible than Shakespeare or the King James Bible of 1611 for spreading and shaping the English language. Last month, I was at the bedside of a woman in her final moments. She asked me to read from the BCP. I read, "Hear what comfortable words our Saviour Christ saith unto all that truly turn to him." She smiled, then said, "Oh, the comfy words. I so love the comfy words."

March 24

This is Holy Week. Holy Thursday, Good Friday, the Easter Vigil, Palm Sunday — when we commemorate the most important events in the life and death of Christ. Easter as a season begins immediately afterwards. It's a busy time. Today I've five home communion visits, a person to see at the hospital, and then one of our Holy Week services. It's a forty-minute drive to my church and I just realized that the man in the car alongside of me is waving. We're doing 110 kilometres an hour, so I'm not sure that a conversation is in order. Then I see that he's pointing to my collar, making the sign of the cross, and giving a thumbs up. I smile back and then he moves on, accelerating to what must be at least 130, which is hardly a first-class commercial for Christian behaviour.

There are obviously lots of candles in churches and at Easter there are more than usual. My church is old and has lots of wood, so the risk of disaster is enormous. Our local fire-chief always looks concerned when he tours the place, and when we agreed to replace open flames with battery-operated candles, he said he'd sleep easier at night. At the Easter Vigil, people hold small candles and lean them when they're trying to read the words of the hymns in the darkened church. That means dripping hot wax. Or worse. "I once saw a woman's hair set alight by the person standing next to her," explains my colleague in a tone that indicates this is hardly the first disaster he'd seen. "People really ought to be more careful in church." I'm bald but still see the advantage of the electronic alternative.

When people ask me about the importance of Easter, I recommend various books and authors but also suggest movies. I know some fine, inspiring Christians who won't go near what they dismiss as "those silly Jesus films," but I disagree. Very few of them are especially bad and some are downright helpful. Not, however, Mel Gibson's *The Passion*. It's more medieval caricature than ancient truth and while Gibson boasts of its accuracy, it has characters speaking the wrong languages, wearing the wrong clothes, and behaving in the wrong way. The crucifixion in the film is far more of a Renaissance painting than a Roman execution, and most damaging of all is that the essence of the story is lost, and Jesus's humanity completely forgotten.

It's hardly surprising that the film industry constantly retells the Jesus story. It is, after all, "the greatest story ever told." That, at least, is what the title of the 1965 Biblical blockbuster contends, the one with Max von Sydow as an incongruously Germanic Jesus, the obligatory Charlton Heston as John the Baptist, and John Wayne almost spoiling the not-at-all bad production as the Roman soldier at the close of the movie who intones in a western drawl that "He surely was the Son of God." It's not easy to make an inspirational Jesus movie, in that we already know what will happen. For example, the nasty Romans are not going to catch the family and slaughter the prepubescent Jesus.

Risen, released in 2016, is little different, a more accomplished, grittier attempt to say something new. Joseph Fiennes plays Clavius, a Roman tribune who, after crushing a Zealot rebellion, is sent by Pontius Pilate to find out what really happened to the body of Jesus. Fiennes also played the reformer Martin Luther in a half-decent biopic that had about the same limited exposure as *Risen*. He's always capable, and in this film, he finds Jesus and sees him ascend into Heaven. Pilate now wants Clavius captured, and the rest of the movie is taken up with our poor Roman evading his former comrades, helping the disciples escape, and trying to reconcile his cynical paganism with what he has seen with his own eyes.

Hail, Caesar! is a bitingly honest, clever, and funny film about the inner workings of a Hollywood studio in the midst of making a movie about the crucifixion. The religious content, then, functions as mere background. Jesus doesn't figure largely, and he's certainly not presented as godlike, but in one beautifully constructed scene, Catholic and Greek Orthodox priests, a Protestant minister, and a rabbi meet to discuss the planned movie and whether they can approve of it or not. It's genuinely funny.

There's long been debate about which interpretations are acceptable and which are not. Martin Scorsese's *The Last Temptation of Christ* (1988) is an adaptation of Nikos Kazantzakis's 1953 novel of the same name and is an original and affirming account of Jesus's struggles with fear, reluctance, sexual desire, and depression. So controversial was the film considered, however, that a right-wing Catholic group attacked the Saint Michel theatre in Paris where it was being screened with a potassium-chlorate and sulphuric-acid device, injuring thirteen people. Other theatres suffered tear-gas canister and stink-bomb attacks, graffiti, and bomb threats.

Godspell, an adaptation of the off-Broadway musical, was released in 1973; it caused predictable outrage from the usual quarters, as did *Jesus Christ Superstar* the same year. Both were sincere efforts to readdress a figure who, in the early '70s, was still considered beyond criticism by most people in the West. *Godspell* probably has better songs and more Christian relevance but alas, as with so many movies of that era, it's difficult to expunge all of the annoying hippieness from either musical.

The Miracle Maker in 2000 is a disarmingly charming and surprisingly moving stop-motion animation film about Christ seen through the eyes of a terminally ill girl living in Capernaum. It depicts scenes that are not recorded in the Gospels, but animated characters can get away with all sorts of things. It has been, sadly, too quickly forgotten.

Some of the best depictions of Christ have been on the small rather than the large screen. *Jesus of Nazareth*, a 1977 television miniseries featuring Robert Powell and a star-studded cast, with direction by Franco Zeffirelli and script from Anthony Burgess, still holds its place as a penetrating account of the life of Christ. One of its advantages is that it's more than six hours long, thus allowing everybody concerned to explore the Christian story properly.

There's also a BBC television film called *The Passion* that is difficult to find but beautiful, moving, and authentic. But if I could point someone to a filmic interpretation of what Easter means, I'd recommend a British television comedy and drama called *Rev.* Starring Tom Hollander and Olivia Colman, it's a three-season show that chronicles the life of a Church of England priest in inner-city London, not too far from where I grew up. The whole thing is essential viewing, but the final series in particular is effectively the Passion, a metaphorical account of Holy Week through the life and troubles of a good, decent, flawed Christian minister. If I had my way, I'd show the whole thing to every seminarian and have them write essays about it.

Then there's Monty Python's *Life of Brian*. Confusion, extremism, religious pedantry, failure to grasp the message, and laughter.

Humour is big in the Gospels, if only people would understand it. There were demonstrations back in 1979 when the movie came out and it was banned in certain places. But Jesus isn't mocked and what the Python team offer is a rejection of collective foolishness, herd mentality, and not listening when truth is spoken.

April

April 1

It's April Fool's Day, so everybody is on guard for the latest prank. Most of them are obvious, but I'm taken in easily. Or am I?

It was a week-long clergy retreat in a remote British monastery, and I was there with three friends. We each had a small room isolated from the rest of the community. They lived in rooms that were connected to the church while we were in an annex a five-minute walk away, and it was always bitterly cold at 3:00 a.m. Still, we'd committed to observing the prayer life of the monks and they rise at 3:15 a.m. to begin the seven periods of praise ("Seven times a day I praise you," Psalm 119:164). Within a few days we found it almost impossible to rise that early but still made the effort. The monks retire at 8:00 p.m., but we couldn't fall asleep at that time. This meant that we were disorientated and that our rest was broken and confused.

On the night before April 1, my "friends" decided to organize a joke. I fell asleep around 9:00 p.m., but they'd stayed up, having agreed to take the following day off. Without my noticing, they'd switched off my alarm, which had been set for 2:50 a.m., and then altered the time on my phone. I'd only been asleep about two hours when they started banging on my door. "Mike, get up! We're going to be late for the 3:15 a.m.!" I reached for my phone; it said 3:10

a.m. and yet I was certain I'd only been asleep a couple of hours. When I opened the door all three were standing there, pointing to their watches. They told me to put my coat on and that they'd meet me in the church. I threw cold water over my face, brushed my teeth while simultaneously getting dressed, and rushed off. It was freezing cold, very dark, and I tripped twice. But I got there in time.

Eyes half-closed, sitting in the pew, waiting for the monks to enter in that magical way of devout silence, broken only be the sound of their breathing and the sweep of their robes. But they didn't come. Ten minutes later and no community. There must be something wrong. And that was about as much time as it took for me to realize that I was several hours early, sitting alone in an empty church close to midnight. I wandered back to my room, to find the three of them sitting round a now half-empty bottle of Talisker whiskey, bent double laughing. I too took the next day off and worked hard on the concept of forgiveness.

April 2

I stop off on the way to church to buy some groceries and in the car park there's one of those totally pointless encounters where two cars are trying to get into the same parking spot. It's not even that crowded today, but pride has taken hold, and this particular spot is apparently golden. My own car is only a few yards away and as I walk past the confrontation, the doors of the other two cars open and both drivers get out. It's at times like that I wish I'd worn a scarf, but it's obvious that I'm a priest and I can see that the people in the suddenly gathered crowd expect me to intervene somehow. Duty, and fear of shame, overcome cowardice and worry, and I step forward and for some unknown reason shout, "Have either of you two got the time? I'm really late!"

Shocked by this bizarre interjection and both men clearly reluctant to become physical, they swear a little, get back into their cars, and drive off. Yes, Christian peace-making has won the day!

I look round and the small crowd begin to applaud. "Oh, it was nothing," I say, "nothing at all." "We're not clapping for you," a woman at the front says, "we're clapping for the cop who has just walked up. They saw him and got lost." I suddenly notice the man in uniform, feeling pathetic because I thought I'd stopped a fight and embarrassed because the people who were clapping knew that's what I thought. I look directly ahead and don't turn around until I'm driving away myself. As I do, I look in my rearview mirror and observe the crowd talking to the police officer and laughing.

April 4

Mary came to see me last summer. She has Parkinson's disease. "It's not just the damned Parkinson's," she says, "but that I'm so lonely. I've been divorced for years, no children, and I just don't have any friends. I'm depressed, it all seems pointless, I know I'm going to get worse, so I've decided that I'm applying for MAID." That's Medical Assistance in Dying. Mary was eventually dissuaded from ending her own life by a group of us at church who organized a support group, helped her with some minor money problems, and simply made her life feel less bleak. Thing is, if she had gone ahead and made an application there's a very good chance it would have been accepted.

I've long been an advocate of a highly limited, strictly controlled form of assisted dying, but zealots on both sides of the debate make it a very difficult subject to discuss. Rather like abortion in that regard. Working a great deal with the severely ill, I've seen too many cases where people plead to be allowed to go, can't take the pain and the medical intervention anymore, and live in constant fear of dying alone and in fear. I've also seen young people who think that life is darkness, older people who are convinced that they're burdens on their family or that all of their savings are being spent on care homes when the money could go to their children, and people like Mary. I'd always assumed that a mature, genuinely compassionate, and humane medical and legal system would never allow those people to be helped to die, but I'm no longer convinced that is the case.

Canada introduced MAID in 2016; more than forty-five thousand people have now ended their lives this way. In 2021 there were more than ten thousand cases; the following year the rate had increased by 30 percent. There's no indication that the increase will stop, and a staggering 4.1 percent of all deaths in Canada now are due to MAID. There are countless horror stories about the apparent abuses to the system but it's often difficult to know whether they're genuine or apocryphal. I do know personally of at least one doctor suggesting, some would say recommending, MAID to his patients. In British Columbia last year, fifty-two-year-old cancer patient Dan Quayle opted for MAID because the province's medical system simply let him down. His partner Kathleen Carmichael said, "The oncologist would come in and say, 'We're pretty backlogged right now so hang in there.'"

He didn't.

Canada's public health system is under siege financially and politically, and palliative care is one of the hardest hit sectors. Although official reports of MAID deaths show that many of those who took advantage of the system had received expert and long-term care, they also reveal a number who either didn't receive acceptable levels of help or weren't made aware of what was available, especially in terms of pain control. Family doctors are the first line of help for the sick and it can be incredibly difficult to find one.

There's another issue. Some advocates are arguing that mental illness should qualify a sufferer for assisted death. This is deeply worrying, and anyone who works with those enduring psychiatric challenges knows their connections with poverty, abuse, and homelessness. To consider mental health as a criterion without addressing the horrors that may have caused the sufferer to despair is downright terrifying. Indigenous leaders in Canada have also spoken out about this because native people are often over-represented in this area. Could it be that what was conceived as a policy to ease suffering could become yet another weapon with which to condemn the poor and marginalized?

April 9

I read of yet another street-preaching Christian confronted by the police. Someone called the cops with an allegation of a homophobic hate crime, the police arrived and explained the complaint, the missionaries filmed the whole thing, conservative websites pounced on the story, and alleged free-speech advocates made a fuss. And the Gospel was advanced not one inch and quite probably took a beating.

The evangelist defended himself by claiming that all he was doing was preaching his religion. Then he insisted that "The Bible says in the book of John, chapter three verse 16, For God's love of the world he gave his one and only son so that whoever, whatever person — homosexual, drunk, liar or a prostitute — believes in him shall not perish and have everlasting life."

That isn't what it says. The reading is, "For God so loved the world, that he gave his only begotten Son, that whoever believes in him should not perish, but have everlasting life."

That being said, the police can certainly be over-zealous, just as some people can be extremely intolerant of anything even remotely linked to Christianity. In Britain an entirely innocuous Gospel singer was warned by a policewoman that she had no right to be performing where she was. The cop, who also poked her tongue out at the camera, was a volunteer officer, and her superiors apologized for her actions.

I certainly understand a desire to speak about God, and there's a noble tradition of engaging the street, but is this about sharing the good news or searching for soft oppression? Having viewed numerous videos of anti-abortion activists breaking bubble zones around clinics, it's clear they know that the police will ask them to leave, and that they are determined to be arrested.

Expression of faith should never be a rant, and it's downright dishonest to reduce it to a handful of strident opinions about equal marriage, women's reproductive rights, and misunderstood eschatology. We need to attract people to church, and we all struggle with finding new and effective ways to do that, but it confirming preconceptions of intolerance is not one of them. I've been criticized in the past for questioning these megaphone martyrs. How can a priest, I was once asked, not defend Christians when they're heckled or hassled merely for preaching? Actually, it's precisely *because* I'm a priest and a Christian that I withhold my support. I care passionately about opening the door to show the world Jesus, and there are all sorts of methods we can use to open that door, but much as I try, I can't see this type of street-preaching as being one of them.

April 12

There's another bout of hysteria about the alleged paedophilia epidemic. As a father of four, I can't imagine anything worse than the sexual abuse of children, but I simply don't accept the panic that's out there. A few months ago, a movie called *Sound of Freedom* was released. Jim Caviezel (Christ in Mel Gibson's *The Passion*) starred as Tim Ballard, a former government agent who rescues children from sex traffickers. The critic Sam Adams wrote perceptively for the online magazine *Slate* that it "arrived in theatres surrounded by a cloud of innuendo put forth by its star and its noisiest right-wing supporters — conspiratorial insinuations about who doesn't want this story to be told and what real-world traffickers are really up to."

Indeed, Caviezel has spoken of "the whole adrenochrome empire," describing the substance as "an elite drug that they've used for many years" that is "ten times more potent than heroin" and "has some mystical qualities as far as making you look younger." He claims that adrenochrome can only be obtained from adrenalin glands in a living human body, leading to the abduction of children. This rubbish has its origins in a QAnon belief that powerful, international figures intent on "resetting" the world, controlling people, and destroying religious freedom are also kidnapping little boys and girls. That was the lunacy behind Pizzagate in 2016, when thousands believed that a paedophilia ring led by those at the highest levels of the Democratic Party was operating out of a Washington restaurant. More than a million messages were sent on Twitter supporting this fantasy, eventually leading to employees being harassed, and a shooting and then arson attack.

There's always been a strong dose of homophobia involved, with the old canard of gay men being groomers, in spite of all the facts and evidence. Facts and evidence, however, are the last things relevant to conspiracy theorists. The trans issue magnified the paranoia, and it's been pushed into the mainstream by a new generation of right-wing politicians. When Florida's Parental Rights in Education bill was being debated, Governor Ron DeSantis's press secretary Christina Pushaw wrote that anyone who opposed the legislation was "probably a groomer." In 2020 on NBC, Donald Trump spoke of his supporters who were "very strongly against paedophilia and I agree with that. And I agree with it very strongly."

As outrageous as these people and their statements may be, they have enormous influence on the gullible. Bizarre ideas about super-wealthy and secretive cabals imposing godless liberalism, fears of children being sexualized or stolen, a terror of change are all empowered by the increasingly media-savvy Right, whether secular or fundamentalist Christian. The disorder may be unique in details but not in theme. In medieval Europe, antisemitic libels accused Jews of kidnapping and killing children so as to use their blood, usually for the Passover ceremony. Pope Innocent condemned the blood libels as early as 1247, but they continued even as late as the last century and led, inevitably, to pogroms and murder. Scratch the surface of modern conspiracy theories and antisemitism often appears, but today the accused are usually singled out not by race but by ideology, including politicians and public figures considered to be left of centre, or even people who support vaccinations, abortion rights, LGBTQ2S equality, or climate justice.

It's particularly tragic as children increasingly suffer in a culture of poverty, food insecurity, and forced migration. Ironically, those roaring about "paedophile rings" tend to ignore the real perils children face and are often opposed to legislation that may actually help them. Child abuse and human trafficking are genuine problems and have to be taken extremely seriously, but baseless and hateful hyperbole only worsens the situation and has to be condemned by conservative leaders who consider themselves to be moderate and responsible. They may not be to blame themselves, but their failure to speak out simply won't do. I genuinely fear that violence will occur, and judging by the temperature, volume, and numbers of the far Right, that violence could be of the worst possible kind.

Death is a constant for a priest, but even though it causes pain and grief, there's an expectancy and a natural inevitability when it's the passing of someone who had led a long life. Early death is different and much more difficult to cope with. The worst of all in my experience is suicide, especially when it involves young people. A teen suicide has just occurred and there's little that a priest can do or say to help. Beyond the pain of the parents, siblings, and family is the guilt that people feel. "If only we'd been there," "If only we'd been better and more loving." In this case that's far from being the truth; everybody involved had tried their best and been very loving and caring. But when someone is convinced that the pain of life — often a result of mental illness — can only be dealt with by ending that life, there's little than can be done.

I've lost friends to suicide myself. I'll never forget one of them, Jimmy, leaving a note in which he apologized for any harm his actions may have caused. I still feel tears in my eyes when I remember that.

May

May 2

Pentecost is usually in May, sometimes early June, and is one of the few times when we're allowed to wear red in church. Red is the colour of fire and represents the tongues of flame that we believe covered the apostles. It's also associated with the Holy Spirit, and with the qualities of passion, love, and enthusiasm. So the altar frontal is red, as are the chasubles (sort of holy ponchos) worn by priests, and our stoles. These are the sashes worn by clergy — deacons diagonally, priests around the neck. Red was the colour of the stoles we were told to wear when we were ordained; we were allowed to personalize them, so I put a crest from Canterbury Cathedral on mine to symbolize my English birth and upbringing, and another from Trinity College, University of Toronto, where I'd studied for my Master of Divinity degree. I had planned to sew a Tottenham Hotspur badge on, too, but my wife gave me one of her quizzical looks when I suggested it, so there is no Tottenham badge on my red stole.

Anglicanism is a *via media*, a middle way, and at our best we take what works from both Catholic and Protestant traditions, including in how we regard the saints. This is an issue at the moment, because a second miracle attributed to fifteen-year-old Carlo Acutis has been confirmed and the boy is on the way to being made an official saint: the first millennial saint. The teenager lies in an Assisi church, dressed in running shoes and jeans and visible through glass. Passing pilgrims walk by and make the sign of the cross. There's also a live website feed. I went on it this morning and was told "33 watching now" and "80,100 subscribers." I also saw a woman posing for a photograph in front of the entombed Carlo. Next to her was a sign that read, "No photos."

The local archbishop says he hopes people who come to pray at the tomb will "open themselves to the light of the Gospel and have a profound experience of faith." I prefer to believe that we can find the light of the Gospel less in the public display of a deceased teenager than in — well — the Gospel.

Carlo Acutis was born in London in 1991. His family returned to Milan when he was very young; he died tragically from leukaemia in 2006. Loving and generous, he worked with the unhoused and defended his vulnerable classmates. He was also a daily communicant who built a website to document various miracles. That website is being highlighted by the Vatican, and Acutis is being spoken of as a patron saint of the internet.

He definitely said saintly things, telling his poor mother, "Mom, don't be afraid. Since Jesus became a man, death has become the passage towards life, and we don't need to flee it. Let us prepare ourselves to experience something extraordinary in the eternal life." The church hopes that such sentiments will inspire other young people in their Christian faith. Perhaps they're right, but my own experience working with teenagers is not as straightforward. They struggle with a complex, nuanced, and challenging world. Yet there's no denying that Acutis has a significant following, which is why Rome initiated the canonization process four years ago. The Medical Council of the Congregation for Saints' Causes found a Brazilian child allegedly cured of a rare pancreatic disease after praying to Acutis, and a twenty-one-year-old Costa Rican who had a miraculous recovery after a life-threatening cycling accident. Formal sainthood could take place as early as next year.

In medieval Europe, canonization could be proclaimed by popular opinion. If the Roman crowd were large and loud enough, a saint was named on the spot. This resulted in some dubious nominees; ambivalence about the process has continued ever since. There are some truly noble, inspiring people on the list but also others more sinners than saints. It's a measured process these days, but politics and public opinion are still significant factors. Pope Francis may be the holder of an ancient office, but he understands, or is advised by people who assume they understand, media and modernity. Most saints are people who died in their maturity, and the younger ones are usually from an era that has limited relevance to young people today, which is something the Roman Catholic hierarchy has repeatedly emphasized in the last few days. Acutis, they say, is different. To an extent that's true, although his mother speaking proudly of her son playing on his Game Boy proves once again how transient fashion can be.

I've no idea if the miracles attributed to Carlo Acutis are authentic. In fact, I've no idea if any miracle is genuine or the product of wishful thinking or coincidence. Some Christians argue that the age of miracles ended long ago, but I honestly don't know. I do know that part of me reacts quite badly to the idea of saints being named like this, and certainly of people lining up to stare at the body of a boy who died at such an early age. What concerns me is that there is something too considered and calculating about the idea of "a saint for a new generation" at a time when the church is struggling to hold on to that very generation.

May 4

A funeral today for a man who was clearly loved, in that almost two hundred people are gathered here. He was in his late eighties, hadn't suffered at the end, and the tributes describe someone who had relished life.

In the midst of all the tears, a young relative comes to the podium and says that we have to remember that the man they are mourning loved to laugh and to tell jokes. She then repeats the last one he'd told her. "A girl goes home and tells her mum that she was with her friends and that they were playing numbers. 'The others counted to five, but I could go to seven. Do you think that's because I'm blond?' Her mother says that it could be. A week later the girl comes home and says, 'Today the girls were reciting the alphabet, and they could get to D, but I got to F. Do you think it's because I'm blond?' The mother says it could be. A week later she comes home again. 'Mum, today we were at the swimming pool and the girls lifted up their tops and they were very flat-chested, but I lifted mine and I was very buxom. Do you think that's because I'm blond?' 'No,' says the mother, 'it's because you're thirty-seven.'"

I don't think there was a person who didn't laugh out loud. Politically incorrect perhaps but funny, and it broke the tension and allowed people to grieve in the way he would have wanted. After the laughter had stopped, I went to the microphone and said, "Actually, I collect jokes that I can tell in my homilies at church. But that won't be one of them."

May 6

There's been another case of what is now known as "cancel culture." As nauseating as the slogan might be, those who throw it around do have a point. While the revolution has to breathe and the complacent and the comfortable might deserve a shaking, there are times when even the most righteous campaign can go too far. It's a theme that will unwrap and find a balance. What irks me is the frequent hypocrisy of so many of those who complain about it. First, it was the Right who successfully played this game for generations, with the Left very much the newcomers. If you doubt me, consider the odious Joe McCarthy, the Roman Catholic Church's *Index Librorum Prohibitorum* ("List of Prohibited Books"; that little beauty wasn't abolished until 1966), or the various progressive voices squeezed out of mainstream culture and argument, especially in North America.

Then there's the personal. Until eleven years ago I was on the Right, especially the Christian and socially conservative Right. The details of my "epiphany" aren't important here, but I've ended up more of a progressive. When I moved my position on some, though far from all issues, I found myself a target. Thousands of emails, death threats, attacks on my family, calls for my wife to leave me, accusations that I was a child abuser, and allegations that I was a thief and a fraud who had only changed his views for money. That was especially odd, in that the same people organized boycotts of advertisers so that newspapers and radio stations would fire me. Credit where it's due: it worked.

I lost five regular newspaper columns, dozens of speeches, a book contract, two radio shows, and a television hosting position. There are genuine conservative defenders of free speech who encourage a whole range of opinions if they're well expressed and within the frame of civilized comment but my goodness, they're in a minority. Voltaire didn't actually say, "I might disapprove of what you say but would defend to the death your right to say it," but he did sort of think it. And at the same time, he benefited from the profits from slavery and spewed such antisemitism that centuries later, the Nazis would use his work in their exhibitions.

May 7

One of the delights of my priestly life is when I'm asked to perform a baptism. Sometimes the ceremony is for babies being held by their parents, but often it's requested by mature people who have come to know Jesus Christ as adults and long for this sacramental bonding into God's family. I welcome every one of them. I suppose I even welcome Russell Brand, who has made the news because he too was baptized. He announced to his millions of online followers that he felt "incredibly blessed" and "nourished." I'm delighted for him and hope that he emerges as a true follower of Jesus, committed to loving his enemies, standing with the poor and the marginalized, and putting others before himself.

But there's more to it than that. Baptism involves transformation, a different life, and what we might think of as a great, glorious coming clean. This new covenant is not just for us but to us; in other words, it's not something that's passive but for an adult is an indication of action and movement, and it also demands humility and contrition. Sins are forgiven, but there needs to be proof that the truth of those sins — errors or wrongs if you prefer — has been understood and accepted, otherwise it can all resemble a politician's public tears. Have lessons been learned, have we paid a price, are we trying to repair damage done? Accepting Jesus means accepting what he demanded of us, and that's not easy.

Brand has been accused of sexual assault, rape, and emotional abuse by four women and has also been interviewed twice by the police under caution for what are thought to be other alleged crimes. One of his accusers was aged sixteen at the time of the incident. Brand denies the charges, arguing that while he was "was very, very promiscuous," he only had consensual relationships. It would therefore be absurd to expect him to admit guilt where he claims there is none. But whatever the legalities, he has clearly hurt people deeply. If he has apologized for it, I haven't seen it.

Nor have I witnessed any indication that he's a changed man. What I have seen is Russell Brand focusing on Russell Brand. "Something occurred in the process of baptism that was incredible, overwhelming, literally overwhelming because I was obviously underwater and it was the River Thames." And "Like it says in Galatians: that you can live as an enlightened and awakened person." That's not all that Paul's letter to the Galatians says. His epistles, the entire New Testament, and the teachings of Jesus aren't just another form of self-help or the latest wellness technique. Yet Brand writes that he is "a person that has in the past taken many, many substances and always been disappointed with their inability to deliver the kind of tranquillity and peace and even transcendence I always felt I've been looking for."

So he's found the right drug, the fix that works, the cure for his turmoil. While Christianity does indeed bring peace, it teaches less that we should "feel" better about ourselves than that we should "be" better because of our belief. Yet that isn't always the case, and faith is sometimes used to justify paranoia and panic. It's significant that conspiracy theorist Alex Jones, one of Brand's loudest defenders, wrote to his more than two million followers on X: "The Lord works in mysterious ways. God bless Russell Brand and his powerful transformation. Free humanity stands with him and with God. Christ is KING!" This is the man who claimed that the 2012 Sandy Hook school shooting, when twenty young children were killed, was a hoax. The families of the victims won nearly $1.5 billion in legal judgments against him. The money has not been paid.

May 19

Someone stops me in the street to discuss religion. Happens more often than you'd think, perhaps because I almost always wear my clerical collar in public and also because I'm sometimes recognized from television or from my columns and books. This man is upset about the non-scientific or antiscientific nature of religion. I tell him that the history of Christianity is actually one of great encouragement of scientific research and has been responsible for many of the most important scientific advances. I mention Francis Bacon, Kepler, Copernicus, and Newton, and then I describe the work and faith of Max Planck, Kelvin, Louis Pasteur, Alexander Fleming, and Gregor Mendel. But what about Galileo? he asks. They always do. I reply that that was not the church's finest moment but nor is it entirely what the popular view would have us believe. For example, Galileo's patron for much of his work was a cardinal who became the Pope. I'm about to go on at greater length when he suddenly says, "Yeah, okay, but could you give me fifteen dollars for a bottle of wine."

May 24

One of them, Gabby, came to my church. In her mid-forties, intelligent and alert, with some minor mental-health challenges, she was covered in a plastic sheet to keep her dry in the rain and was wheeling a large suitcase containing all that she owned. She'd slept several nights in local bus shelters, sat in libraries or coffee bars during the day, and spent her time phoning or visiting places to find work or a room to stay in. She spoke highly of the local police, who were supposed to move her along when they saw her sleeping outside but knew she had nowhere else to go. When I drive in to church early on a Sunday morning, I always see people asleep in shelters, and this is in one of the more affluent cities in Canada.

She asked if we could help her, explaining that she'd contacted all the shelters in Burlington and they were full. I said I'd try anyway and called them again myself. She was right.

I then extended the search to Oakville and Mississauga. Nothing.

Surely Hamilton had something. Rejection after rejection. "I'm really sorry," said one worker who answered the phone. "You can call others but I'm telling you that there are just no vacancies."

Another shelter manager told me to look further afield. "Perhaps try Owen Sound." I said that it was two hundred kilometres away, that Gabby had no money and no transport, and if she managed to get there and found no place to stay, she'd be in an even worse state than she already was. We ended up giving Gabby some cash, which we seldom do, and some cards to use at local stores, which we often do. I felt like such a failure.

I know people who are working, even working full-time, but can't afford an apartment. Because shelters are so full, they use tents to attain a minimal degree of privacy and a little sleep. I asked one of the people we help if Toronto, the big city, was any easier. "Yes and no," he replied. "I have a job here, even though the money isn't great. I can't risk losing that. There are more shelters and places to sleep in Toronto but more people too. There's another thing," and he takes a deep breath. "There are angry people in some of those places and to be honest, they frighten me. I'd rather be cold than scared." But being cold is a genuine danger in Ontario as we approach winter. Cities issue weather warnings and open public venues for those living outside, but that's temporary and inadequate. A few hours unprotected in January temperatures can be fatal.

I can't pretend to have all the answers, but I know that many good and kind people aren't aware of how common the unhoused problem is. They don't realize how many of those we might assume go home each night to warm and safe homes actually spend the night on the streets. Shelters help but we need more of them, and the demand will only increase. They're also a temporary response when what is needed is a long-term solution. Affordable housing is vital and that means a fundamental shift in government policy at all levels. I'm just not sure if the political and public will is there anymore, or if it ever was. We're a prosperous province in a prosperous country, and we even sometimes boast of being "the greatest country in the world." I'm not sure how Gabby and the others would respond to that, but I do think that any nation should be measured on how it treats its most vulnerable.

May 26

I'm not a fan of American football but sometimes sport bleeds over into public life, and even religion. Kansas City Chiefs' kicker and three-time Super Bowl champion Harrison Butker addressed the female graduates of Benedictine College in Atchison, Kansas. In his speech, the twenty-eight-year-old Roman Catholic spoke of a "deadly sin sort of pride that has a month dedicated to it" (an obvious reference to Pride Month, celebrating the queer community), said that some Catholic leaders were "pushing dangerous gender ideologies onto the youth of America," warned of "the tyranny of diversity, equity and inclusion," and criticized U.S. President Biden's defence of the 1973 Roe v. Wade decision. He also said to this assembly of highly intelligent young women, "Some of you may go on to lead successful careers in the world, but I would venture to guess that the majority of you are most excited about your marriage and the children you will bring into this world."

There's been a great deal of pushback and anger, but that's been countered by plenty of support and enthusiasm, including a major spike in sales of Butker's jersey. The NFL, however, merely said that he was speaking "in his personal capacity" and that "his views are not those of the NFL as an organization." And so another hero of the Christian Right took his place onstage. There was another comment, and one that has received less attention that these obviously crass statements. "Congress just passed a bill," said Butker, "where stating something as basic as the biblical teaching of who killed Jesus could land you in jail." For those not familiar with its rancid implications, this statement concerns the idea that the Jews killed Jesus, a canard that has led directly to centuries of antisemitic persecution, murder, and expulsion. Moreover, the "bill" to which he's referring, the Antisemitism Awareness Act, has nothing to do with criminal law, cannot lead to incarceration, and isn't directed at individuals but at schools that receive federal funds.

Yet it's not merely playing to racism that is so concerning about Butker and his allies, but their sheer ignorance of basic Christianity. No one group, ethnic or otherwise, is responsible for the crucifixion; all of us are. Jesus came preaching peace and love, and humanity rejected him. If you don't get that, you don't get the Gospels. And it seems to me that a number of people today who complain about how they're losing their rights to abuse others don't get those Gospels at all. I never thought I'd write this, but perhaps the last words should go to Mel Gibson, hardly the most progressive of Christians. In *The Passion* he filmed his own hand hammering the nails into Jesus. "I'm first on line for culpability," said the actor and director. "I did it."

June

June 3

A parishioner comes to see me in quite a state. She's extremely upset that yet another artist has depicted Jesus in a purposely and pointlessly malicious way, either to insult or to attract attention. The woman isn't angry or mean-spirited, more hurt and confused. To her, and to most of us who see the church on a daily basis, the influence of Jesus is positive and liberating. How, she asks, should we react?

It's a very good question. For many years it has been open season on Christianity in art, literature, television, film, and theatre. There are many reasons for this, one being that the consequences are either positive or harmless. There's prestige in mocking what is still considered to be part of the establishment, and in spite of what some may claim to be the case, the possibility of physical violence or career damage is minimal. The obvious contrast here is with critics of Islam. I've interviewed Salman Rushdie, author of *The Satanic Verses*, who was attacked and almost murdered, as well as Kurt Westergaard, the Danish cartoonist who drew the picture of Muhammad wearing a bomb in his turban and lived the rest of his life under police protection. There are many others who have felt the sting of religious extremist intolerance.

But that being said, the Christian response to any controversial issue is based not on the failings of others but on the call of the

Gospel. We're made to celebrate the heart set free and to relish all that is given to us, and that certainly includes art and literature. The vocation of the Christian is not to limit but to broaden our vision, not to be reactive but pro-active. The church has been the handmaiden of creativity, whether it be the magnificent art of the Renaissance, or the literature of Dostoyevsky and Tolkien. Even the mockers are products of Christianity, whether they realize it or not. The very freedoms, the very openness, that allows mockery of the faith is a product of the precise Christianity that is under siege. Such authentic liberty would never exist in an atheistic society — witness the former Soviet Union, Maoist China, National Socialist Germany. The paradox that these ostensible radicals fail to appreciate is that the licence they enjoy is a consequence of that which they despise.

As for the works themselves, we have to differentiate between them. Anything that obliges me to think deeper about my faith is to be welcomed, even if it does sometimes hurt. Nobody welcomes a trip to the doctor, but it doesn't mean we don't have to go. My response in a perfect world would be to politely ask the artist, author, or museum director out for lunch or coffee to explain what the Christian faith means, to talk about how fellow believers in so much of the world face daily persecution, to outline the horror of blasphemy laws and how we as Christians feel when what we hold so dear is insulted for no apparent reason. It might work; it might not.

June is Pride Month, and as a Christian who has for more than a decade defended LGBTQ2S people and their full place in the church, it means I'll be asked to write certain things and also defend my arguments to Christians who disagree with me. I'm also straight, married for thirty-six years, and with four children — none of them gay, contrary to what my critics claim. If any of them were, it wouldn't matter to me and shouldn't matter to other people, but it does. Unfortunately, Pride Month provides an opportunity for conservative Christians throughout the world to take to their pulpits and podcasts to explain how pride is a sin, the Bible condemns homosexuality, and that the allegedly traditional family is under concerted attack.

These allegations are untrue, a betrayal of what the Bible teaches, and completely lacking in the grace and empathy that's the quintessence of the Jesus story. Actually, scripture seldom mentions same-sex relationships; there are a mere handful of references to the subject in the almost eight hundred thousand words of the Bible. The Old Testament never once speaks of lesbianism and Jesus doesn't address the subject at all. The vital point about the Bible is that it can be taken literally or seriously, but not always both. It's far too profound to be reduced to a simplistic manual for modern manners. The greater point is that too many Christians are looking through the wrong end of the theological telescope, missing the central point of Jesus's teachings, and searching for digressions that serve to justify their prejudices. Christian homophobia is far more a sociological than a religious construct.

If Jesus stresses anything in his ministry, it's the injustice of legalism and scriptural pedantry, the harm caused by judgmental hypocrisy, and the danger of rejecting the outsider. His mantra is love, endless and eternal love, and a permanent revolution of grace and justice. Not easy of course, but then anybody who thinks that practising true Christianity is easy has missed the point. C.S. Lewis said, "Next to the Blessed Sacrament itself, your neighbour is the holiest object presented to your senses." Sometimes those neighbours wave rainbow flags or love their same-sex partner. If anybody thinks that the argument is over, they should see my emails. I'm regularly contacted by young Christians from Christian families who are struggling due to parental angst. Their mothers and fathers aren't cruel or abusive, they love their children, but they've spent decades consuming traditional teaching on the subject and they genuinely believe that their beloved child is destined for hell.

June 4

I attend a morning Mass at a Roman Catholic church. I don't receive communion there, not because I agree with the Catholic Church's restrictive policy — only baptized Catholics in good standing are qualified — but because I respect the decisions of another church. This notion of the table being only partially open is one of the things that pushed me away from Roman Catholicism. But there were so many more. Even Pope Francis, progressive in many areas, makes some outrageous comments and decisions. Nor has he been completely open about his past. Jorge Mario Bergoglio has long been accused of not doing enough during his country's junta government to protect two of his fellow Jesuits who worked with the poor and were political radicals. Both were arrested and tortured. One of them, Father Yorio, would later claim that Bergoglio had betrayed him. There's also the Chilean clergy sex-abuse scandal. It was a dreadful case, yet when the Pope visited the country, he angrily criticized Chilean Catholics protesting the appointment of a bishop who had hidden the crimes of another priest. It was outrageous and led to clergy working with abuse survivors to publicly correct the Pope. He has an undeniable intellect and a heartfelt care for the poor and the exploited, but there's also a worrying and, I suppose, Jesuitical defence of some of his less than constructive actions. Regarding women's ordination, he has been terribly disappointing but says it's because clericalism is a problem and making women priests would be potentially damaging and that Mary is more important than Peter, and female mysticism is unique. Oh please!

June 6

The anniversary of D-Day. I know one veteran who was on the Normandy beaches. He's almost totally blind but still mischievous and sharp, and whenever I see him in church, he has a teasing smile on his face. He asks me if I know about what happened to Canadian soldiers at the hands of the 12th SS Panzer Division during the Second World War. I said I didn't. He told me the story and then I did my own research to confirm it. It's a harrowing tale.

In the days following the allied invasion of France, between June 7 and 11, 156 Canadian soldiers were executed after surrendering. That figure represents one in seven of all Canadians who died in the first week after D-Day. It's a quite extraordinary statistic. This includes the killing of individual unarmed and often wounded men as well as the mass execution of prisoners, who were protected under the Geneva Convention and were anyway no threat to their captors. The perpetrators of these atrocities were soldiers of the 12th SS Panzer Division (Hitler Youth), but only one of those responsible, Colonel Kurt Meyer, was ever charged. In other words, the crime went largely unpunished. The murders began on June 7 when a number of North Nova Scotia Highlanders and the Sherbrooke Fusiliers were captured after the battle of Authie. That night eleven Canadians were taken into a garden and shot in the head. Seven more were murdered in the early hours of the following morning.

On June 8, sixty-four Canadians, many from the Royal Winnipeg Rifles, were taken prisoner. They were taken to the Château d'Audrieu, under the command of the 12th SS Panzer, and forty-five of them were slaughtered in separate batches. After the battle of Bretteville-sur-Odon, thirty-six Canadian prisoners, mainly from the Cameron Highlanders and Regina Rifles, were executed, some shot at point-blank range and others by machine gun fire. On June 11, Canadian troops from the 2nd Armoured Brigade and the Queen's Own Rifles were defeated in an attack close to the village of Le Mesnil-Patry. Their losses were heavy, and many were wounded. After the defeat, a number of the prisoners were shot by their captors. In one incident, a Canadian was shot dead but his two comrades survived, escaped, and were able to report what had happened. These survivors weren't alone. As the killings continued in the following days, the Germans tried to hide their crimes, but the allies were advancing and found increasing evidence and heard more testimonies from witnesses. Several weeks later, a Canadian newspaper headline announced, "Canuck Soldiers Murdered!"

The campaign following the invasion was intense and costly, however, and there was little time to investigate war crimes while attacks and counterattacks were happening daily if not hourly. By the time the Nazis surrendered, their obscene behaviour toward civilian populations, and the full horror of the Holocaust, was emerging, and the fate of 156 young Canadians was, if not forgotten, relegated to secondary status. Many, likely most, of the SS grenadiers who had been involved were dead. There were still official inquiries, written accounts, and the commander of the 12th SS Panzer, Kurt Meyer, was eventually put on trial in December 1945. Canadian and German soldiers, and French civilians, gave evidence. Meyer was sentenced to death, but on appeal this was reduced to life imprisonment. The Canadian public was outraged, the Soviet Union considered demanding he be sent to Moscow to face a trial for alleged war crimes when he'd served on the eastern front, but instead Meyer was sent to a prison in New Brunswick, Canada. He asked for clemency in 1951, in an era when the U.S. and Britain were looking to West Germany as an ally against Soviet expansion. He was returned to Germany, released in 1954, became active as an apologist for the Waffen SS, and died of natural causes in 1961, lionized by many in Germany.

There are memorials in Canada and in Normandy to the victims of the Normandy Massacres but not many, and the names of the victims are mostly forgotten. Fifteen thousand people attended the funeral of Kurt Meyer.

June 7

I've got Covid-19. I was in one of the first groups to receive the original vaccine because I fell into the right age category when the pandemic hit, and while I may have had the virus last year when I was in England but wasn't tested, this time is worse. I'm tired, cough a lot, but otherwise fine. It really isn't too bad. Thank goodness I followed up on the vaccines whenever possible. Or, to put it another way, thank God for vaccines. Yet far too many Christians oppose the Covid-19 shot, and many of them are opposed to vaccinations in general. When the virus first became a problem in North America, a poll by the U.S. Public Religion Research Institute found that 45 percent of white evangelicals said they'd refuse the vaccine, and the indications are that this number has remained fairly static. In Canada the percentages seem to be lower, but the problem remains. In those early days, a Christian conservative MP named Derek Sloan sponsored a petition before the House of Commons claiming, "Bypassing proper safety protocols means Covid-19 vaccination is effectively human experimentation." It received more than forty-one thousand signatures.

The Christian opposition to vaccines then and now is multifaceted. The most ideologically plausible, if still bizarre, objection comes from those convinced that embryonic stem cells have been used in the development and manufacture, and in some cases that may be true. Yet even the Vatican has said it's "morally acceptable" to receive a vaccination that has used cell lines derived from aborted fetuses, due to the "grave danger" of the pandemic.

But Pope Francis is not popular with Catholic conservatives, and they look to alternative leaders such as Cardinal Raymond Burke, who has said that the virus "has been used by certain forces, inimical to families and to the freedom of nations, to advance their evil agenda … These forces tell us that we are now the subjects of the so-called 'Great Reset,' the 'new normal,' which is dictated to us by their manipulation of citizens and nations through ignorance and fear." That hero of the Catholic Right has in the past tested positive for Covid-19.

Other forms of Christian antivaccine hysteria are drenched in "hidden agenda" fantasies, conspiracy theories about the state and secularism, and eschatological mania. There is a global battle, it is said, between the remnant of authentic Christians, be they Catholic or evangelical, and the Godless forces of government, media, and business. Covid-19, and the vaccine response to it, is all part of the plan to control and dominate. Covid-19, runs the antivaccine narrative, is either a hoax or, if real, nothing more than a mild flu. If the latter, it has been exploited by plotting governments and elites to close churches, remove freedom of religion, and impose vaccines. Donald Trump, always eager to echo fundamentalist rhetoric, said that some states had closed places of worship while allowing "liquor stores and abortion clinics" to stay open.

The obsession with conspiracies isn't confined to Christian conservatives, of course, and is typical of any subgroup that sees its authority under threat by a world it can't accept or understand. The consequences, as we know only too well, can be fatal. In the Christian context, the obsession is tied in with polemics about Armageddon, the end times, and the notion that vaccines contain the "mark of the beast." This nonsense is supposedly from the Book of Revelation, where the Antichrist is said to tempt Christians to mark their bodies. That's a childish misreading of the deeply complex final book of the New Testament, as much poetry as allegory, and demanding a nonliteral approach. Problem is, literalism is at the broken heart of the antivaccine theocrats.

June 10

On a radio show the interviewer asks me about writers I admire. I list a lot, including Arthur Conan Doyle, the creator of Sherlock Holmes, Dr. Watson, Professor Challenger, and Brigadier Gerard. She seems surprised, but I insist that he was not only a great writer but a fascinating man. He was, I said, a confirmed spiritualist who went to his death still defending the honesty of a Yorkshire schoolgirl who claimed she had taken photographs of a group of gossamer-winged, wand-waving pixies. The photos still exist; the story was exploded many years ago. I'm certain that she thought I was joking.

I wasn't. Conan Doyle's life was dominated not by detective writing but by a conviction that the supernatural was a reality, and that through a belief in, and understanding of, spiritualism, our lives could be made complete and abundantly meaningful. He wrote more than twenty books on the subject. A cartoon of Conan Doyle has him with his legs manacled to a tiny Sherlock Holmes, the smoke from the diminutive detective's meerschaum pipe enveloping his Gulliver-like creator. "Stop writing letters to me about Sherlock Holmes!" he wrote in June 1922. "It is of limited interest. Ask me, please ask me, about Spiritualism, about what really matters."

He always maintained that he had two birthdays: May 22, 1859, when he was delivered from his mother's womb, and November 14, 1893, when he became a member of the British Society for Psychical Research. Born and raised a Roman Catholic and educated by Jesuits, he rejected his religion almost as soon as he left home.

There's a short film of him, which is remarkable because he died in 1930. It's shaky, the cameraman has no notion of framing and continuity, and it is often a little out of focus, but it manages to convey the delightful essence of the man. He grins a great deal, talks to his dog, flirts with the camera with a confidence rare for filmed subjects back then. Some of the ten minutes of the piece are concerned with Sherlock Holmes, but the bulk is spent on spiritualism. Any questions as to why he embraced the movement, why he believed so much of its content when even some zealots were more selective, is answered therein. A serenity comes to his face when he discusses spiritualism.

He toured the United States and Canada on several occasions and was fascinated by a poltergeist sighting in Montreal. "The electric lights were switched off at untoward moments, and the pictures were stripped from the walls. Twice the husband was assaulted by pillows until his incredulity had been buffeted out of him. Prayer seemed of no avail." He was also moved and shaken by the psychic immensity of Winnipeg! The magician and escapologist Harry Houdini was yet another devotee of spiritualism and he and Conan Doyle became close friends. They eventually fell out because Houdini thought that his friend was being taken in by frauds.

He was always prepared to stand for causes he believed in, even if that made him unpopular. He defended Sir Roger Casement, who had spied for the Germans during the First World War so as to aid the Irish Nationalists. Calls for Casement's blood were ubiquitous, especially when it was discovered that he was gay. Conan Doyle believed that he was mentally ill and shouldn't be executed. He received threatening letters accusing him of treachery and became a public hate-figure for a while but refused to back down from his defence of Casement.

June 12

There really is a lot of nonsense being written at the moment about the religiosity of modern Russia, and the place of the Orthodox Church in Vladimir Putin's disastrous invasion of Ukraine. While we can't be sure of the precise motives of the Russian despot, the idea that this political and humanitarian catastrophe is somehow due to theological imperialism is absurdly far-fetched. That, however, is what's being suggested by some newly minted experts on the region. Putin, they claim, is devout, sees Kiev as the Slavic Jerusalem because it's where Christianity began in the region, and is angry that in 2019 the Ukrainian Orthodox Church declared independence from its Russian Orthodox sibling. That decision, by the way, was supported by Bartholomew I of Constantinople, nominal head of the international Orthodox Church. In response, the Russian church separated from the greater Orthodox world.

Forgive the pun, but it's all invincibly Byzantine. I first discovered that back in 1988 while cowriting a CBC documentary to commemorate the one thousandth anniversary of Christianity in Ukraine. There are divisions within divisions, not made any easier by *Kievan Rus* being the name of the land from which Russia, Ukraine, and Belarus all originated. Putin has certainly increased the influence and profile of the Orthodox Church, but Russia itself isn't a particularly observant nation. More than 80 percent of Russians may claim to believe in God but very few ever attend church. A mere 10 percent spend their Sundays in worship, which is low even by European standards, and a fraction of the rate in the U.S.

As for Putin's personal piety, accounts vary. His mother was a devoted believer, and his own sense of Russian identity is likely deeply woven into a sense of Orthodoxy, which is true for many of his compatriots. It's tempting to say that Christians don't command armies that kill innocent people, but we all know that that's not always the case. Whatever the reasons, it's extremely unlikely that the war is purely a holy crusade for Kiev. This is more about NATO than the New Testament. It's worth remembering that even Joseph Stalin, a former seminarian but a convinced atheist, curtailed his venomous persecution of the church in 1943 in an effort to increase patriotic fervour against Nazism.

The Russian Orthodox Church itself is divided on what is happening. In an almost unprecedented display of defiance, more than 250 Orthodox clerics issued a statement in which they said that the people of Ukraine "must make their own choices by themselves, not at the point of assault rifles and without pressure from either West or East." The letter continued, "We call on all opposing sides for a dialogue because there is no other alternative to violence. Only an ability to hear the other side can give us hope to get out of the abyss our countries were thrown into several days ago. Let yourself and us all enter the Lent and Easter in the spirit of faith and love. Stop the war."

Patriarch Kirill, the head of the Russian church, remains a firm supporter of Putin, whose rule he once described as a "miracle of God," and in those words he speaks for a number of his fellow clerics. For the priestly class, the wounds left by the Soviet Union's suppression of religion will never fully heal, and any leader who subsidizes their new cathedrals and prays in their churches will always be revered. Christian nationalists in the West have long applauded Putin for his socially conservative policies and support for what they regard as traditional family values. Franklin Graham, son of Billy and one of the world's leading right-wing evangelicals, praised him for "protecting Russian young people against homosexual propaganda." As Fox News commentators and their comrades like to say, Putin is the antithesis of woke and that, they conclude, is a direct product of his faith.

That does a disservice to the Orthodox Church, with its many centuries of beauty, sophistication, and suffering. It's flawed but also profound and diverse, and to reduce it to American slogans is numbingly banal. The five wounds of Christ are replicated in the holy wounds of Ukraine. Invasion, murder, lies, abuse, and terror. A country bleeds for us, not as Christ who some of us regard as the Messiah, but as a living obstacle, a heroic barrier to the ambitions of a malicious and cruel leader who exploits and oppresses his own people in his lust for power and land. It will not end with Ukraine, as history has repeatedly taught us. Some in the world wash their hands of all this, preferring to do nothing while the noble victims die in their place. Others genuinely lament what is happening but don't intervene because they think it would be too dangerous for them.

July

July 6

I haven't played cricket since I came to Canada in 1987. I've played some rugby and soccer over here but never cricket and, to be honest, the rugby and football was a few years ago now. As a young man I was a half-decent wicket-keeper — the position behind the batsman — so when I was asked to play in the Anglican Cricket Tournament in Brampton, Ontario, I said I would. Problem is, wicketkeepers have to dive, jump, and run, and what I could do in my teens, twenties, and even forties, I can't necessarily do in my mid-sixties. It was a very hot day, everybody was enthusiastic, I proudly took my place, and all went well. There was a commentator broadcasting on a PA system and after one surprisingly athletic dive when I caught a loose ball, he said, "Very good stop there by the keeper."

I suppose it went to my head. The next ball was also quite wide, I dived, and then felt a shooting pain in my right hamstring. That was my day done. I limped off, feeling very old and rather pathetic. I'd never pulled a hamstring before, and didn't even know I had one. My leg healed, of course, but did my self-confidence? When I told my former professional athlete son if he thought it was my hamstring, he asked, "Is it the bit at the back of your leg below your bum and above your knee?" I said it was. "Yep," he said, "it's the hamstring. It'll heal, no sweat." I like to think that it was caring rather than contempt in his voice but I'm not entirely sure.

Cricket and the Anglican Communion have a connection of course, because the Church of England was part of the British Empire, and as the empire expanded it took with it its national church and its national sport. The influence of baseball means that the game never took hold in Canada, but in India, Pakistan, the West Indies, Australia, New Zealand, and other former British-ruled countries, it's almost a religion. The difference is that while enthusiasm for the church has declined, the appeal of cricket is as strong as ever. Which is why this tournament of a handful of teams is strongly South Asian and Caribbean in composition, with just a few pale, old types like me.

I recovered, but I'm not sure if Donald Soper ever did. Lord Soper was a British Methodist minister, president of the Methodist Conference, a member of the House of Lords, and in the 1950s and '60s, one of the best-known and respected Christians in the world. What isn't so widely known is that as a young cricket enthusiast, and before the body padding that we now have, he bowled a ball that hit a batsman above the heart and killed him instantly. Soper never forget what happened, and it partly shaped his faith and his Christian pacifism. It's "traumatic to be responsible for killing someone," he said, and for a period struggled with depression and religious doubt.

Questioning what we believe, whether it's a religious faith or a secular ideology, is crucial if we're to remain emotionally stable and mature. The religious world, like the political one, has decayed partly due to the invincible self-confidence and the overwhelming arrogance of believers — Left as well as Right, observant or atheist. Being able to see when we're wrong and, even better, being able to apologize isn't easy. It isn't supposed to be, but it's fundamental to any Christian faith worth the name.

Soper's Methodism still exists but it's a shadow of what it was. It's long been said that Britain's Labour Party owed more to Methodism than Marxism, and certainly the radical, social democratic tradition of the British Left was strongly influenced by Christian socialism. The same is true of Canada, with former New Democratic Party leader Tommy Douglas, a hero of the Left, being a Baptist minister. This compassion and commitment to social change comes directly from Methodism's founder, John Wesley. I remember as a sixteen-year-old watching a television series called *The Fight Against Slavery* about Christians in the late eighteenth and early nineteenth centuries who battled slavery in Britain and its empire and eventually triumphed over an evil that was defended by far too many establishment Christians at the time. John Wesley's beliefs were powerful forces behind the abolitionist struggle. "Do all the good you can, by all the means you can, in all the ways you can, in all the places you can, at all the times you can, to all the people you can, as long as ever you can," said Wesley. I wonder how many people reading that today would consider it fanciful and naive?

July 9

A young woman I've known for many years asks me out for coffee. I know that this must be about something important because such an invitation is a rare pleasure. I'm also sure that she wouldn't have asked me before I was ordained. It's that collar again.

When we meet, she seems nervous and unsure. Could she ask my advice about something personal? Of course. Without being specific, she wants to know my opinion of abortion. I explain that in a perfect world it wouldn't exist but that this isn't such a world, and that while it's a difficult issue, women have the right to control their own bodies. But, she asks, aren't Christians always opposed to abortion? I reply that this phenomenon is relatively recent, and that it wasn't until the 1960s and the emergence of a more open and liberated society that evangelicals coalesced politically around the issue. Not all evangelical Christians of course, but certainly most. It was a reaction to what they perceived as moral decay but what most other people regarded as progress.

The Roman Catholic Church, I continue, was stirred into action a little later by the Roe v. Wade ruling in 1973, and similar provision of reproductive rights in Canada. Abortion is still central to mainstream Catholicism, so it wasn't difficult to mobilize a traditionalist wave of Catholic media, activists, and politicians, and to form alliances with Protestant brethren to fight the issue. But many individual Catholics disagree with their church on abortion, and mainstream Protestant churches such as the Anglicans have a more pragmatic approach.

I then discuss what is says in the Bible. Jeremiah, writing around 600 BCE, curses the day he was born. "Cursed be the man who brought the news to my father, saying, 'A child is born to you, a son,' making him very glad. Let that man be like the cities that the Lord overthrew without pity; let him hear a cry in the morning and an alarm at noon because he did not kill me in the womb; so, my mother would have been my grave, and her womb forever great." It's a cry of deep sadness and despair, but it doesn't imply prohibition. It's not this Biblical reference we hear from the anti-abortion movement, but another quote from Jeremiah. "Before I formed you in the womb, I knew you, and before you were born, I consecrated you; I appointed you a prophet to the nations."

This has become a slogan for anti-abortion activists, largely because it's one of very few direct allusions to life before birth that they can find. However, it has to be read within its context. It's a reference to a special plan for one man rather than a general approach to biology and reproduction, a reference to the vision of God and the importance of Jeremiah and his mission. It's also Biblical hyperbole, written in a language that constantly uses rhetoric and poetry to make a point.

Another oft-used quote, and another that mentions the womb, is in Psalm 139. "For it was you who formed my inward parts; you knit me together in my mother's womb. I praise you, for I am fearfully and wonderfully made. Wonderful are your works; that I know very well. My frame was not hidden from you, when I was being made in secret, intricately woven in the depths of the earth. Your eyes beheld my unformed substance. In your book were written all the days that were formed for me, when none of them as yet existed."

Lyrical but, again, what exactly is being said? This passage is surely about God's power, and it doesn't say anything that is at all specific or exclusive to the fetus. The Christian belief is that God knows all, knows us, knows who and what we are. Knows, remember, the woman who is desperate, poor, young, and alone — who can't afford to have a child, who was raped or abused, who is terrified, who has no health care, who is crying out, after much thought and consideration, to terminate her pregnancy. Knows the goodness and purity in her heart and the harshness of those who condemn. Put simply, the ancient, Biblical statement that God is all-powerful has no relevance to the rights women have over their own bodies.

The other Biblical text sometimes used to oppose abortion is the story of Elizabeth, the mother of John the Baptist, in the New Testament. When she meets with Mary, the mother of Jesus, the following is recounted in the Gospel of Luke: "When Elizabeth heard Mary's greeting, the child leaped in her womb. And Elizabeth was filled with the Holy Spirit." It's a central verse for Christians, linking as it does Jesus, who is the Messiah, with John, who was the Baptist and would introduce the Son of God to the world.

But it doesn't have anything at all to say about the subject of abortion. First because it merely describes movement in the womb and second because this is a reference to people who are not ordinary, not usual, not as the rest of us. This is a poetic illustration of the link between Jesus and John, a scriptural ballad telling of what is of the eternal, the humanizing of salvation. It's not a guide to female reproduction.

The anti-abortion movement certainly doesn't always display a Christ-based love for others. The humiliation and degradation inflicted on women outside of clinics is genuinely shocking. I've watched protesters howling at vulnerable women walking into clinics, calling them "murderers" and predicting that "God will not forgive" them. Then there are the people who insist on distributing millions of leaflets showing graphic, bloody pictures of abortions, even putting them through the front doors of private homes where it's likely that children will see them.

I talk about the claim that anti-abortion activists are peaceful, and say that some have been responsible for stalking, kidnapping, assault, attempted murder, murder, arson, even bombings. Anti-abortion extremists are considered a domestic terrorist threat by the United States, where most of these incidents occur. There have also been attacks in Australia, New Zealand, Canada, and elsewhere. In the U.S., at least eleven people involved in providing abortion services, including four doctors, two clinic employees, a security guard, and a police officer, have been murdered. In 1992, Henry Morgentaler's clinic in Toronto was hit by a firebomb following several less successful arson attacks. In 1997, Manitoba doctor Jack Fainman — an obstetrician who performed abortions — was shot by a sniper as he sat in his living room. Winnipeg police called the attack "terrorism against doctors." He survived, but his injuries meant that he could never work as a doctor again.

My long speech is done, and I have to admit, I feel proud of myself. I ask her if this has helped in any way, confident it has. "To be honest," she says, "I'm more confused than ever."

July 11

I've forgotten how many times people ask me about hell. How can a loving God allow it? According to a leading atheist journalist, he was told by Pope Francis in an interview that hell, in its traditional definition, didn't exist. Rob Bell, a former evangelical church leader, argued a similar point in his book *Love Wins*: "Has God created millions of people over tens of thousands of years who are going to spend eternity in anguish?" he asks. "Can God do this, or even allow this, and still claim to be a loving God?"

Almost all major religions, monotheistic or otherwise, have featured some hierarchy of reward and penalty after death. The specifics are debated — some faiths describe endless torture, others a place for introspection — but the concept of consequences in the afterlife has been a constant. In a book all about hell, Marq De Villiers argues, mischievously but not entirely unfairly, that Old Nick has gotten a bad rap over the centuries: Satan was originally seen as a more neutral figure within the church, one who reflected the darker side of human nature that must be struggled against. During the Middle Ages, de Villiers writes, "Satan more and more took on his sinister shape as chief villain and chief prisoner, locked away by God yet with the ability to indulge in unlimited malice."

One theory as to why the idea of hell became so prominent is that much of Europe's ruling class — and the church with which they sometimes enjoyed a symbiotic relationship — was terrified that the fear of earthly punishment was insufficient to assure order among the populace. But this thesis assumes that the certainty of hell produces good behaviour, and that clearly wasn't the case; the devil and his instruments, after all, were readily accepted at times when massacres and murders were common.

Other religions have been less concrete in their approach to damnation. For Buddhists, the closest word for hell would be *Naraka* — a place where some beings go because of poor actions taken in life. *Naraka*, however, is never said to be eternal, and its residents are free to leave after a few hundred million years. Meanwhile, Islamic texts describe a place called *Jahannam*, where sinners will be punished physically as well as spiritually. There is a lot of fire in *Jahannam* — indeed, in many religions, flames are linked to ideas of purging and cleaning, as well as being bloody painful.

Judaism is the least punitive and precise of the Abrahamic faiths on the issue of hell. Jewish texts instead speak of *Gehinnom*, which is more like a purgatory — a place where the dead are judged according to their earthly actions and made aware of their failings. Interestingly enough, most adherents to Judaism didn't even imagine a retributive afterlife until they were exposed to Hellenic ideas around 400 BCE. Ancient Greek thought was multifaceted but envisaged a gloomy place below the underworld of Hades called *Tartarus* where torture and suffering were meted out to a deserving few. When Jews became steeped in Greek culture, they picked up some of these beliefs around retribution, and as the diaspora travelled, its theology was influenced accordingly.

Not all religious leaders spent time thinking of the many ways people could and should be punished. Some African and Australian cultures were rare in not having any specific language for hell or any concepts of post-death judgment either.

As we understand more of the world, our beliefs tend to change — hell, therefore, is partly a product of us. We see that in the way secular society has dragged more progressive churches away from the need for voluntary goodness, which, I'd argue, is far more synchronized with the original teachings of Christ. It's not that people no longer believe in the difference between right and wrong; rather, hell may have fallen out of favour precisely because people believe in making decisions out of love rather than legalism.

For myself, I regard hell as a place without God, something which is entirely the result of our own choice. Do we desire eternity with God or without? Both options are open to us. As to the details of that choice, I think it's likely far less absolute and formal than we think. A person who does good, loves, forgives, tries to make the world a better place, may have said yes to God without even knowing it.

July 17

This day in 1944 Jane Haining died. Her place of death was Auschwitz. Her name may not mean anything to most people, and that's the case with regiments of Christian martyrs not as glamorous or medieval as the great and grand names. She was a Scottish Presbyterian missionary who moved to Hungary in the 1930s to teach, and to teach mainly Jewish children. Not to convert them, just to care for them and love them. She refused to leave when the war started. Later, when the Nazis occupied Budapest and things got worse, she knew their inevitable fate. And knew hers as well. She ended her last letter with the words: "There is not much to report here on the way to heaven." She was forty-seven years old.

When I think of people like Jane my heart breaks, but I'm also so encouraged. Horrors are committed in the name of the church, and for that matter every religion and pretty much every cause and creed. That's human nature, that's human brokenness, perhaps that's even original sin. But there are heroes of the faith as well, and we probably meet them all the time but don't recognize them.

William Temple, Archbishop of Canterbury during the last years of the Second World War and an early opponent of Nazism, said, "Socialism is the economic realization of the Christian gospel." Some might argue that this was a step too far, but when we read of Jesus surrounding himself with those on the economic, political, and social fringes of society, it's difficult to consider the Messiah conservative, at least not as we use the word today. I appreciate that the modern world can seem intimidating to some, but I suspect this has always been the case. There have been so many things to oppose these days: women's liberation, racial awakening, new family structures, protests against foreign wars. Listen to people who worry you, spend time with them, hear their opinions, know them as people. Objectification is un-Christian, in fact the opposite of what we're told in the Gospels. See God and goodness in everybody.

July 20

I so wish that Israel wasn't always in the news but I've a feeling this will be the case for a very long time to come. I always feel a cloud descending when this happens, partly because I've lived in Israel, worked with Palestinian Christians in the peace movement, wrote my university thesis about pre-state Zionist terrorism, know the history and politics of the region rather well, and believe in a ceasefire, a two-state solution, justice for Palestinians, and peace for Israel. I'd always assumed that most of my fellow Christians agreed with me on all this and I continue to believe that the vast majority still do. I've written at length on the problem of Christian Zionism, how it's militaristic, ignores the Palestinian Christian narrative, and at its most bellicose looks to an eschatological bloodbath. But what of the

Christian Left? I'm never comfortable with qualifying Christianity and much prefer C.S. Lewis's use of the word "mere" — which he took from the seventeenth-century theologian Richard Baxter. But while "left" and "right" may be clumsy adjectives, they're useful shorthand. I am a man of the Left, I suppose. So, I was a little surprised today when I was blocked on X by a cofounder of the Red-Letter Christian movement in the U.S. and a prominent left-wing Christian. I'd objected to his reference to the "Holocaust hermeneutic." I found it to be reductive and offensive, especially as I'd grown up being aware of my great-aunt's death camp tattoo.

I'm sure I'll survive that social media excommunication but it's indicative of a genuine problem. The Palestinians have become a cause for the Left, and that includes left-wing Christians. That's understandable, but for Christians there has to be a wider, deeper, more nuanced analysis. One of, perhaps the main, motivation for Israel's foundation in 1948 was the unparalleled agonies suffered by Jews in Christian Europe. Jews left the Arab, Muslim world later and weren't the main protagonists in the early years. Centuries of pogroms, blood libels, expulsions, massacres, and finally the Holocaust took place in a continent that was overwhelmingly Christian. Good God, many of these atrocities were church-initiated, and it's only fairly recently that the wound of Christian antisemitism has begun to heal.

None of this should prevent a Christian from demanding justice and peace in Palestine, but it should inform our approach, understanding, and sympathies. I've also seen a shameful lack of empathy when Christians refer to Jesus as a Palestinian. I appreciate what's being attempted, but we should never forget the horrors that have been caused by the expunging of the Jewishness of Jesus. He was a Jew, a Galilean Jew, with a Jewish mother. To suggest otherwise is not only bad theology and a denial of God's plan but also racially and politically dangerous. I sometimes hear and read things from

Christians that border on the racist and make it appear that the entire Israel/Palestine conflict exists in a bubble without any historical and human context. Colonial settlers? Where were the survivors of the Shoah and later the Mizrahi Jews from the Arab world supposed to go, and why does my paternal DNA go back not to Europe but the Middle East?

Israel and its supporters have used antisemitism as a justification for the actions of a nation-state, false accusations of antisemitism are damaging, and no authentic follower of Jesus can turn away from the slaughter of the innocents. But our commitment is not to a political ideology but to a relationship with God.

July 22

An extremely generous and thoughtful member of the congregation bought me a gift token for a British candy store — or "sweet shop" to be precise. I spent it on enough chocolate to counter my daily statin tablets, which will please my doctor no end. These shops were rare when I came to Canada in 1987, but now places selling British chocolates, sweets, food, and memorabilia seem to be everywhere. They began catering to a small niche market in the 1970s. Back then, before the internet, British Sunday papers would arrive by Monday lunchtime, and such shops were the best places to buy them. It was bit sad really, seeing expats lining up for a newspaper like that. As online news developed and hard-copy papers were less in demand, these relatively few shops branched out into selling food. By the early 1990s, the number of shops selling British chocolate and biscuits had multiplied, and now there must be more than a dozen in Toronto alone. They have names like "British Pride," "Across the Pond," the "Scottish Loft"; the products on offer vary with the seasons but the constants are familiar:

Mars, Double Decker, Twirl, Galaxy, Minstrels, Yorkie, and Fry's Chocolate Cream.

And the menu goes well beyond that. Every type of British cookie (biscuit), often from Marks and Spencer, bottles of Fairy Liquid, Imperial Leather soap, *Coronation Street* and *EastEnders* mugs, football scarves and hats, tea towels picturing various royals, books about the Lake District, and a plethora of *Downton Abbey*, *Doc Martin*, and *Carry On* DVDs. Fox's Glacier Mints, actually much less common in Britain, and Dolly mixtures, also much harder to find in the U.K., are never out of stock.

Why the success? Canada is far less British than it once was, two generations of immigration have changed the country's tastes, and while we're still a monarchy and have the Union flag around, the pull of U.S. culture and commercialism is difficult to resist. It's partly Brits and the children of Brits still longing for things they'd likely never buy if they were in London or Manchester, but most of those queuing up for their Branston pickle have little if any connection to a country they've often never visited. In other words, there's profit in imagination as well as nostalgia. It's comfort-shopping for some, and Anglophilia for others, especially Americans who flood the stores just over the border in Niagara Falls and see Canada as the closest thing to Dibley and Queen Victoria they're likely to find.

For someone like me, it's almost a form of regression. I'd never have gone to these places twenty years ago but, as I age, I grab lifelines from a happy past. While contemporary Brits frequently look to the foreign for glamour or thrill, those living three thousand miles away, British or otherwise and young or old, see the U.K. as offering something special and unique. And, yes, they even buy Marmite and claim to enjoy it.

July 25

Today I'm doing my paradox thing. There are wars everywhere and so I'm spending a day reading, thinking, and praying about Christian pacifism. War has always been with us, but we've never had the ability to inflict such slaughter so rapidly and so easily. The reality is obscene; the potential even worse. But the point is that wars keep occurring not because they're successful but because of the very opposite. Perhaps the most misplaced statement in the annals of armed conflict is that coined by H.G. Wells to describe the First World War: "The war that will end war." Even if wars succeeded in bringing peace and prosperity, there would still be a moral argument against them. But they simply don't.

Very few people regard war as desirable, but the majority likely hold, whether they know it or not, something along the lines of the "just war" theory. The United Nations charter, for example, states, "Only in the inherent right of self-defence against armed attack can a Nation be justified in resorting to military force, without the approval of the Security Council." St. Augustine wrote that war was only morally acceptable if waged to defend the innocent, and today a just war would be based on the principles of right cause and last resort, declared by proper authority, having an appropriate intention, possessing a chance of success and the use of proportionate means.

The pacifist argument, on the other hand, doesn't have much support these days, and the political Left largely abandoned the idea long ago. When they chant "stop the war" they usually mean stop the war against the people they support. One of the few areas where pacificism does still have some support is within Christianity, and even there it's generally a fringe commitment. The Anabaptist tradition is often pacifist, as are the Quakers too. But for the most part, churches see peace as a vital end rather than a valid means.

Yet Jesus told us to turn the other cheek, love our enemies, put down our swords, and that peacemakers will be blessed. He also told his followers to buy a sword, although this may have been metaphorical, and he certainly demonstrated righteous anger when he cleared the Jerusalem temple of merchants and moneychangers. But taken as a whole, and certainly compared to his contemporaries, Jesus was indeed "the prince of peace." The early church was largely, though not unanimously, pacifist, and Christian pacifists won praise during the Second World War by serving as medics on the front line. Although there were others — often political rather than religious objectors — who refused even to work on farms because they regarded it as aiding the war effort.

Immutable pacifism is, whatever the motivation, difficult to live. Refusal to resist violence directed at oneself isn't the same as refusing to intervene when another, innocent and perhaps vulnerable, is attacked. Then again, defending someone against a street thug isn't the same as launching a missile. I honour the memory of those who battled Nazism, but much of devastated Europe was left in the hands of Soviet tyranny, hundreds of thousands of innocent people died, and the Holocaust certainly wasn't stopped. Some would even argue that the Shoah was made more possible by war conditions and the cloud of secrecy. And that particular war is usually cited as the case against pacifism.

Korea was five years later, then Vietnam, several wars between India and Pakistan, Israel and its Arab neighbours, wars in Latin America, Indochina, Africa, the Middle East, and even between Britain and Argentina over the Falkland Islands. That conflict, said Jorge Luis Borges, "was a fight between two bald men over a comb." The number of people, often civilians, who have been killed or horribly injured is in the millions. The soldiers who are killed or wounded are frequently conscripted or in the military because of no alternative jobs — jobs that could be provided if investment went into infrastructure rather than armaments. Beyond the human tragedy is the financial cost. It's beyond reliable calculation but runs to trillions of dollars, and more than enough to build housing and factories, fund medical systems and schools, feed and clothe people. Which would go a long way to remove the very reasons why wars start in the first place.

If you're more comfortable, let's call it hatred of war rather than love of peace, war phobia instead of pacifism. Either way, it's more relevant than ever. So, will I now come out as an absolute pacifist? Let's say I'm a work in progress.

July 26

J.D. Vance is a disturbing character. Eight years ago, he publicly described Donald Trump as an "idiot," condemned him as "reprehensible," and privately compared him to Hitler. Now he's the reprehensible Hitlerian idiot's vice-presidential running-mate. But his transitions go beyond the political. Raised in an evangelical culture, in 2019 he became a Roman Catholic. It's a little surprising in that in his bestselling book *Hillbilly Elegy*, published in 2016, he hardly mentions Catholicism and never more than in passing. The journey toward Rome was evidently a fairly rapid one. There's long been a conservative attraction to Roman Catholicism due to the church's rootedness in ancient tradition, its commitment to unchanging values, and, if we're honest, a certain innate misogyny and homophobia. I was a Roman Catholic for many years and wrote two bestselling books about the Catholic Church, so know that most Catholics don't share in the more reactionary aspects of church teaching. But the ideology is still there, can be seen clearly in the catechism, and Vance knows that better than most.

Because he's no fool and his embrace of Catholicism is as cerebral as it is spiritual. He has, as it were, come home to a place that seemed to affirm his beliefs. I'm not sure, however, if that's what Christianity is supposed to do. If it doesn't challenge us, there's something missing. That intellectualizing of the instinctive, painting a theological veneer over a rusty mindset of regressive politics, took on a particular appeal under Pope John Paul II, and while things have liberalized under Pope Francis, the largely U.S.-based and funded Catholic magazines, think-tanks, and lobby groups are firmly in the conservative fold.

They've been active around women's rights and sexuality, and in 2022 Vance said in a podcast that he "certainly would like abortion to be illegal nationally." He also opposed federal protection for same-sex marriages. That protection was, he said, "a bizarre distraction from other issues."

He's been criticized for using the word "groomer" — a common homophobic dog-whistle — but responded, "I'll stop calling people 'groomers' when they stop freaking out about bills that prevent the sexualization of my children." There's more. Many commentators are convinced than Vance is what is known as a "Catholic integralist," an adherent to an arch-conservative ideology advocating that religious authority should be integrated with political power. This philosophy sits closely with its kissing cousin, Christian nationalism. It's hardly mainstream within the church and not something backed by the current Vatican but is deeply influential not just in the U.S. but also in conservative Catholic circles in Canada. Vance hasn't discussed this but has close friendships with activists and magazines that are identified with integralism and many of his beliefs fall directly in line with their thinking. The Catholic Right in all of its forms, not just integralism, argues that marriage and family are the bedrock of a civilized society, that both are under sustained attack, and that progressive and redistributive economic policies are an intrusion and have to be opposed.

That's where Vance's style of religion slides so neatly into the vacuum created by Trump's moral and political hysteria. It's less that Christian conservatives always agree with the Republican leader than that they view him as providing an opportunity to advance their own beliefs.

It all seems too distant from the immaculate teachings of a poor Jewish prophet wandering around an occupied country with a group of marginalized people, calling for peace, love, human dignity and equality, and the world made anew.

JULY 27

The Opening Ceremony has taken place for the Paris Olympics, and it was spectacular, fun, and weird. Part of it featured an extremely camp montage that according to the planning committee celebrated diversity, but was condemned by some Christians as being an attack on Christianity. It seemed more pagan and ancient Greek than anything else, but some saw it, not entirely unreasonably, as a parody of Leonardo da Vinci's fresco *The Last Supper*. Not so, responded official choreographer Thomas Jolly. "I didn't have any specific messages that I wanted to deliver. In France, we are a republic, we have the right to love whom we want, we have the right not to be worshippers, we have a lot of rights in France, and this is what I wanted to convey."

Bishop Andrew Cozzens of Crookston, Minnesota, and Bishop Robert Barron of Winona-Rochester, Minnesota, immediately went into denunciation mode, with the former stating, "Jesus experienced his Passion anew Friday night in Paris when his Last Supper was publicly defamed. As his living body, we are invited to enter into this moment of passion with him, this moment of public shame, mockery, and persecution." Bishop Barron, frequently on television, radio, and the press, claimed that "France felt evidently, as it's trying to put its best cultural foot forward, that the right thing to do is to mock this very central moment in Christianity."

Frankly, I doubt that the people involved had much of an ideological plan, but even if they did, and if it was supposed to mock Christianity, was this really the best and most appropriate response? The permanent outrage position of too many Christian leaders doesn't help the faith and only enforces the unfortunate belief that we're all killjoys uncomfortable with people having fun. If only a few more bishops would speak out with righteous anger about war and poverty, perhaps the attitudes of the non-Christian world toward us would be more positive.

August

August 1

The trailers for the second and final television series of *Wolf Hall* have been released and they look spectacular. I devoured the Hilary Mantel trilogy about Thomas Cromwell, and the television adaptation of the first two books was superlative. I've been a Tudor history nerd since I was a teenager, and in some ways it was a love for the sixteenth century that made me understand the appeal of history and, in turn, literature and learning. *A Man for All Seasons* was the great Tudor movie back then, and Robert Bolt, who wrote both the original play and screenplay, was a master storyteller. His stage dramas were remarkable, but it was in writing or adapting his or other people's work for the screen that he shone the brightest. *Doctor Zhivago*, for which he won an Oscar, *Ryan's Daughter*, *The Bounty*, *The Mission* … and he was a cowriter of *Lawrence of Arabia*. *A Man for All Seasons* is one the few dramas that has shaped, some would argue distorted, the reputation of a historical figure. Sir Thomas More was known before Bolt's 1960 play, but that and the film in 1966 presented him to a truly international audience.

More was Lord Chancellor under Henry VIII, was the author of *Utopia*, and was one of Europe's leading intellectuals. Perhaps most significantly for his legacy, he was also martyred for his opposition to Henry's divorce and break from Rome and canonized in 1935. For a married layman, a father, a lawyer, a politician, and an Englishman to become a saint is a very rare thing indeed, and there's an enormous and organized devotion to the man. But is that adoration for the authentic Thomas More, or to Robert Bolt's interpretation?

Bolt was the son of Manchester Methodist parents, later a communist, never a Catholic or even Christian in the conventional sense, and was motivated by something entirely separate from piety or faith. For him the play concerned fidelity to an individual's idea of truth, and to what Bolt described as his relentless "sense of his own self." So, in some ways, Bolt's hero is more a quintessential modern, more an enlightenment hero than an unyielding Catholic refusenik. There's an awful lot of "I believe" in the text, an ideological stance that would likely have been something of a problem for More through much of Catholic history.

A counterweight to Bolt's hagiographical account was the school of sixteenth-century history shaped largely by the great Cambridge historian G.R. Elton. He championed Thomas Cromwell, More's nemesis, and regarded Cromwell as one of the creators of the modern state, a warrior of the free and the new. To that world view More was an obstacle, a problem. He detested the man.

Other historians followed, supporters of Thomas More responded, and then several decades later in 2009 came Hilary Mantel's *Wolf Hall* novels and subsequent television adaptations. In her hands, More was transformed from courageous humanist to rigid reactionary, prepared to personally supervise the torture of Protestants in his zeal to maintain Catholic order. He takes new form as a literary snob and an arch-puritan. There's also a powerful thread of a martyrdom complex in Mantel's portrayal, of More virtually seeking death for the sake of his own legacy.

Wolf Hall was hardly popular with More's followers, and Catholic publications have rushed to his defence. There's no evidence that he was intimately involved with torture, and while he certainly accepted the need to burn heretics to death, that places him firmly in the mainstream of religious and political morality at the time. As for his stalwart and ultimately fatal defence of the Papacy, there were numerous Catholics willing to support the early reformation. It's ahistorical to assume that they were all corrupt or cowardly, or that the events of the 1530s were Lutheran. The old brute King Henry slaughtered Protestants as well as Catholics, remained Catholic in his theology, and, along with various bishops and thinkers, was more concerned with creating a national, non-Roman church than a reformed, non-Catholic one. The genuine reformation began with his son Edward VI and was developed by his daughter Elizabeth I.

August 2

As well as being a priest, I'm still a working journalist, and write regularly for a dozen major newspapers and magazines in Canada and the U.K. That gives me a certain profile and also sometimes leads to a heated response. It comes with the territory of course, but social media has transformed the way people respond to that with which they disagree. Twitter, now called X, is in decline, but in spite of various attempts at alternatives it's still dominant, and online comments are even quoted in newspaper articles as valid opinion. I lost almost ten thousand followers when Elon Musk bought the thing, many of them progressive-minded people who had had enough. I don't blame them but was determined to stay on that platform myself. I could still have an influence, especially as a Christian, and especially as a priest.

As a priest, how I respond to hatred and abuse matters a great deal. I'm a realist, and I realize that most of what I write, or what

I say for that matter, is as permanent as a cobweb, and that my influence is limited. But there's no point being falsely modest, and I know how many emails I receive from people all over the English-speaking world wanting to know more about Christianity, sparked into at least partial interest by something that I've written. I write for my diocesan monthly, *Niagara Anglican*, and for the *Church Times* and *Premier Christianity* magazine in Britain, but most of my work is for the secular media. When I write a column with a Christian theme for the *Toronto Star*, for example — and they've been especially generous to me in terms of space and regularity — I reach hundreds of thousands of people. If nothing else, many of them have been obliged to take a second or a different look at organized Christianity.

On social media, however, there are those people who hate what I say with a passion, and what I've discovered is that the extreme Right and extreme Left, militant atheists and militant fundamentalist Christians, can be equally vile both in what they say and how they say it. It's no exaggeration to say that over the years I've received tens of thousands of threats and insults, been abused for being a Christian, for being Jewish, for being too pro-Israel, for being too anti-Israel, and pretty much everything else. A column this year annoyed Sebastian Gorka, former deputy assistant to President Donald Trump, and an extremely high-profile conservative broadcaster. He made a nasty comment about me, and because he has more than a million followers on X, many of them evidently retweeted what he had said. The attacks went viral and for the following forty-eight hours — these things always seem to have that lifespan — I was swamped. There were more death threats than usual, with one delightful fellow sending me a video of his day at the gun range and insisting that he was coming for me.

Everybody has helpful suggestions when this happens. Call the police, sue, leave the platform, and so on, but I'm not going to run away, and I know these situations too well to think that official complaints will make much of a difference. I blocked huge numbers of people but — and this is the point — I never replied and reacted angrily or nastily. I do sometimes mock, but never maliciously, because I try to remember that I represent my church, my faith, and most important of all, I represent Christ. Whether I want it or not, when people see me as a priest, they assume I speak and act for the church.

People have said to me, "Why reply to that person? It won't change them." First, it *does* sometimes change them; I've even had apologies. Second, I'm less interested in how the person I'm replying to reacts than how the countless third parties reading my replies will feel. I know — because I've heard it many times — that people are impressed that when the most hideous things are thrown at me, I respond politely. On a good day, they will conclude it's because I'm a follower of Christ and so take the love, joy, peace, patience, self-control, kindness, and "turning the other cheek" stuff seriously.

I'm also an old hand at it. When I left the Roman Catholic Church twelve years ago and became an active champion of socially liberal causes, I was stunned by the number of Twitter attacks on me and on my family. One woman alleged that I rented my daughter out for sex, another claimed that I had once lost a job because I was mentally ill, yet another that it was being half-Jewish that led me to being "an enemy of the church." I knew, of course, there would be some reaction and ignored most of the garbage, but after one conservative Catholic critic had implied on Twitter that I was a child abuser, I decided to respond. I'll never forget what he wrote back: "This is Twitter. You asked for it."

I'd put myself out there and had to be prepared for lies and libel. I used to spend too much time on X when it was still Twitter, had a verified account, and some famous people followed me. I joined years ago because one of my media employers wanted me to do so, and I remain on the platform because, in spite of the cruelty I encounter, it can be a vibrant means of communicating, a place where I can chance upon people who I would otherwise never meet. At its best, it's a sociological triumph. But what genuinely makes X popular is the hatred and the nastiness. For the platform to work, it needs engagement, and it gets engagement from stoking outrage. The #MeToo movement encouraged women to disclose their personal stories of sexual assault and harassment. But antirape advocates and survivors also found themselves being skewered online for speaking out.

Hatred isn't confined to X, of course. The European commissioner for justice and consumers, Vera Jourova, closed her Facebook account after being exhausted by the relentless trolling (women are often most frequent targets on social media). The platform is so rage-filled that, in 2013, a team of California researchers were able to create a "hate map" of the United States by tracking and aggregating 150,000 homophobic, sexist, and racist tweets over an eleven-month period and linking hate speech to specific locations. The project, according to one of its geographers, showed how social media platforms such as X "have been adopted and appropriated to allow for these ideas to be propagated."

X has also proven an effective tool for public shaming. British author and actor Stephen Fry had more than twelve million Twitter followers. In early 2016, while hosting a major awards ceremony in Britain, he joked that his friend Jenny Beavan, an esteemed movie costume designer, was dressed like "a bag lady." She found his remark funny and said so. Nonetheless, Twitter turned on Fry with pitchforks. He was labelled a misogynist and a hater. The Right called him gay and liberal. For the Left, he was a "fucking sexist." The attacks became overwhelming, and he briefly shut down his account. (He later returned with a far less active page.) "Oh goodness, what fun twitter was in the early days," he wrote on his website. "A secret bathing-pool in a magical glade in an enchanted forest … But now the pool is stagnant. It is frothy with scum, clogged with weeds and littered with broken glass, sharp rocks and slimy rubbish. The fun is over."

Because of its largely uncontrolled nature, X has become the most mainstream forum for those denied a media outlet. In other words, all varieties of fanatics, conspiracy theorists, and eccentrics. The platform is soaked in Holocaust denial, fringe politics, antisemitism, and racism. People usually ignored or unable to be published in respected newspapers and magazines establish major fan bases. A study by Safe Home, an organization of home-security experts, showed that X accounts run by anti-immigrant and anti-Muslim organizations have boomed over the past four years. When challenged about all of this, X's managers and spokespeople say they are doing all that they can to maintain civility and legality. And while it's true that there are sometimes investigations and even suspensions or terminations, this is incredibly rare and very difficult to initiate and achieve.

The libertarian, egalitarian logic behind X's refusal to intervene is the free-speech argument that otherwise powerless individuals are suddenly liberated by the unlocked gates of social media. Yes and no. First, many of the most acidic commentators, especially on the alt-Right, are led by organized campaigns and either begin their social media lives as part of a that campaign or are co-opted as soon as they showed any success. Second, freedom does come with certain responsibilities, both moral and legal. Careers and reputations have been severely dented by Twitter. Sometimes the offending tweets are dumb and outrageous, but the punishment is generally less about the offence than the reaction.

In 2013, Alicia Ann Lynch lost her job after posting a photo of herself dressed as a Boston Marathon bombing victim for a

Halloween party — she put on gym clothes and painted some fake blood on her legs and face. It was stupid, to say the least, but she was twenty-two and hardly a figure of influence. She received death threats, her home address was put on what was then Twitter, and posts called for her to be attacked and abused and for excrement to mailed to her. Someone undertook deep research and found some racy photos of Lynch that were then posted, and she was fired. All of these consequences resulted from a moment of thoughtlessness, an immature attempt to be funny. She closed her account, but it was too late.

Far too often, hatred wins the day on X, because hatred is not a by-product but the very essence of the form. The attacker's cry is "I've managed to be abusive to someone, so I am fulfilled." It's a little like the road rage some people feel in cars, where the weak feel powerful and the cowardly brave, because they cannot see their victim and assume that the person they are attacking cannot and will not ever hit them back. But that's the justification and not the cause itself. What does it say about modern society that such a large proportion of regular users are systemically unpleasant, even repugnant? If we put aside the Nazis and the propagandists, there is still the flippant cruelty that powers the platform and that X refuses to censor.

One answer is that people have always been like this, but before the advent of social media, they didn't have the means to communicate their dark nature to a wider audience. In other words, it's the medium itself that's at fault. Insult has become the new manner of social-media conversation, and thought and reason are seen as weakness. As such, not only would it be against X's commercial interests to control hatred, but it would also contradict the very culture it's helped create.

August 5

A call comes in the middle of the night. A desperately ill woman is close to the end, I'm told. There was very little time so would I pray over her on the speaker phone and give the last rites? Anglicans don't call them last rites, nor strictly do Roman Catholics, but I get the point. I agree and pray at length.

A pause. "She's gone," says her daughter. "She's gone." Another pause and I could hear someone crying. The woman's daughter thanked me; we arranged that I'd visit the next morning. I said I was available at any hour to listen or help and then said goodbye. I then realized that mine had been the last voice her mother had heard. Did my prayers release her, enabling her to let go? Was I, in some way, responsible for her death?

I had a sleepless night of confusing emotions, with guilt refusing to leave the room.

August 7

Mine is a late vocation. Most of my working life was in media, but something was always missing. It's difficult to explain a calling without sounding "holier than thou," but as I aged, I began to wonder whether on my deathbed I'd be happy that my profession had been that of a journalist. Which isn't to insult journalism but to put it in perspective. The movies aren't true; reporters hardly ever change the world. They do valuable work, we would be in trouble without them, but I've never bought the self-reverential approach. But a journalist is what I was, what I still am, and my journey toward ordination was hardly simple. I had doubts, reconsiderations, fears. Surely, I was too old to start over, and what if I spent all those years studying for the priesthood only to be rejected?

What became clear was that there was no alternative. I didn't *want* to be a priest; I *needed* to. To be with people in their pain and suffering. To preach and listen — listen, primarily, to God, who often speaks through the most surprising people. In its authentic form, the church is a community, a divine symbiosis of love, a mutual romance based in Gospel teachings and modelled on the life of Jesus.

August 8

Two visits today. On one of my regular hospital visits a patient asks, "Can we talk about *Downton Abbey* rather than religion?" Sure, I said, I've seen every episode, and who wants to talk about religion anyway? After forty minutes she said to me, "Ooh, I thought you'd be strict and boring, but you're actually not so bad at all." Must remember that one — "Actually not so bad at all."

The next visit was a man in his late eighties. He asked if I'd listen to some thoughts he'd collected. He just wanted to chat, really. "I've no complaints," he said. "The bugger is, I don't think I'll outlive the week." "Yes, you will," I insisted. I presided over his funeral ten days later.

These sessions, with their waves of suffering, stay with you. One night I received a call asking if, in the morning, I'd visit a parishioner who was in very bad shape in the intensive care unit. Of course. Up at 5:00 a.m., I was at his bedside by 6:00 a.m. With his daughter, we watched the dawn break over Lake Ontario — the brotherhood of birth and death. The man thanked me for being there and apologized for the trouble he was causing.

Then off to a care home where I take regular services. These places vary enormously and in some of them are people who, though alone, experience a state of comfortable, if sad, retirement. Not this day. From what I could gather, this group — about thirty, all women — lived with dementia. One lady held a baby doll tight; another shook her head in constant disapproval. The group responded a little to the hymns played on an old CD machine. Traditional and tested prayers, I've discovered, have resonance. I recited them, thanked everybody, and left. At the door, one of the women, who hadn't opened her eyes the entire time, said, "Thank you. You've made my day. My husband was a priest. I loved him very much." Then she closed her eyes again. A nurse said to me, "That's the first thing she's said in a week."

I got into my car and cried.

Pulled myself together, drove off, then received a call about the man I'd sat with earlier in the morning and with whom I'd shared the sunrise. He'd just died. Back to the hospital to speak to his family. I tried to explain what I believe about death, but I never impose and never insist. I once knew a cop who left the church because his evangelical partner would try to convert alcoholics living on the street and would be overjoyed when they said that they were "born again."

Meet people in their pain but never take advantage of it.

August 9

I'm in Montreal for a speech and always enjoy being here. I'm not sure how many Montreal residents know that the city was once home to the Nazi foreign minister Joachim von Ribbentrop, convicted at Nuremberg for his role in the Holocaust and executed on October 16, 1946. He recorded in his memoirs that he was "cordially received" by "Canadian friends," but of course this was in 1910, long before his involvement with Nazism. He worked at the Molson's Bank and was listed on the 1911 Canadian census records.

He did well, was promoted, and fellow banker Walter Boucher wrote that "Von Ribbentrop was a young man of outstanding ability. He was so anxious to learn the Canadian banking system that he used to stay until the last man left the office at night. He spoke immaculate English, and gained the confidence of all with whom he came into contact." He moved to Ottawa in 1913, became a popular figure in Ottawa society, and only returned to Germany the following year when the First World War started.

I doubt that very much would have changed if Ribbentrop had remained in Canada, because he was a follower rather than a leader, and the racist ideologues and obsessives who formed and led the Third Reich would have done their work without him. But I can't help but wonder. A friend told me a story that when Ribbentrop was German ambassador to London, his son studied at Westminster School. While there, he urged the other boys to beat up the Jewish students. Appalled at the suggestion, they beat him up instead. I do so hope that it's true.

August 11

I visited a hospice. They can surprise people, because they don't usually look the way we assume they will. This one was more like a quiet suburban home. By the bed was a photo of the woman I was there to visit, a mother and a wife; the photo was only a few months old. In it, she looks so fresh and happy, so full of life and hope. She's so transformed now, so emaciated from the cancer. Death's propinquity is easy to detect, and I knew it was near, could almost feel it. I spoke and prayed, hoping my words would make a difference. I wanted her to be at ease and not feel fear. I always begin with that — you're safe, you're held, you're loved. She passed soon afterward.

"Will I ever get over it?" her husband asked, no tears left to shed at this point. I told him that, in my experience, it's not about getting over death but getting used to it. No use pretending it will be easy.

August 16

Today I think about Roger and wish that everybody could have known him. He was a very ordinary sort of man, the type that is perhaps made fun of. He lived alone, dressed modestly, was quiet and unassuming, and had led a very uneventful life after retiring from the public service in Britain. I met him back in August of 1973, when I was fourteen and had an annoying and arrogant teenage self-regard. My grandpa had suffered a heart attack, and I went with my mum to visit him in hospital. Mum didn't drive, so after seeing grandpa, we stood at the bus stop in the cold. Suddenly, a large car stopped, and the small, middle-aged driver wound down the window and said, "I can take around five or six passengers home if you like. No charge. Anybody interested?" We all looked at each other, all wondering if there was a catch, but gradually we climbed in. The driver asked us where we wanted to go, took us home, wished us a happy evening, and drove off. That was Roger.

I later discovered that he spent almost every day driving around that hospital, trying to ease the discomfort of those visiting friends and family who were ill or even dying. On Sundays, however, he was at his local Methodist church, because Roger was a devoted Christian. Each Christmas he would spend his entire monthly pension on food and drink and then distribute it to the homeless. I found this out because there was a feature on Roger in the local newspaper after he died. It also said that there were so many people at the funeral that the crowd spilled out of the church and had to watch and listen though the open doors.

August 18

There's been a lot of coverage this month over the fact that in late July, a sexual assault case against Canadian megachurch leader Bruxy Cavey was dismissed due to court delays. I know and like Cavey, and while he denies the charges, he does admit to adultery. His church, the Oakville-based Meeting House, was perhaps the largest and most successful megachurch in Canada but lost numerous members and even suspended services after it could no longer obtain abuse insurance. There had been several earlier cases involving other clergy at the church.

This story originally broke just three years after the death of Ravi Zacharias, one of the most popular and influential preachers and Christian authors in the world, who lived for many years in Canada and attended what was then called Ontario Bible College. He was posthumously exposed as an abuser of several women. One survivor of his crimes said that Zacharias called her his "reward" for a life of Christian service.

Shortly before this, the Ontario Court of Appeal made legal history by dismissing two main components of an appeal by the Roman Catholic Basilian Fathers of Toronto against the awarding of $2.57 million in damages to a sexual abuse survivor. This was the highest amount ever awarded in such a case. The victim was Rod MacLeod, his abuser the late William Hodgson Marshall, who sexually abused MacLeod more than fifty times. Marshall had been convicted of abusing seventeen young people over his thirty-eight-year career, and there are accounts of other priests accidentally walking into areas when the abuse was taking place and simply leaving, closing the door, and keeping the crime to themselves.

But sexual abuse isn't confined to any one region or religion, and while we pride ourselves in this country of being an egalitarian society, we're just as respectful of elites and authority as the Americans and the British. That's acutely pertinent, because society's perception of a priest or minister as being set apart, special, and uniquely significant sometimes provides a hiding place and cover for abuse. That type of attitude exists throughout the world, but as someone who has lived in three counties, I believe it to be especially noticeable in Canada.

Then there's the formation and training of the clergy themselves. Many denominations are desperate for clergy, and this can lead to cutting corners. I'm confident that at Trinity College, University of Toronto, and in my various church internships, I received a first-class training, where issues of power, sexuality, and boundaries were regularly discussed. We're re-trained, are tested, and police-checked on a regular basis. I know that this isn't replicated in every branch of the Christian faith, and I've sometimes been astounded at the lack of guidance and supervision.

There's an understandable need for younger clergy, for people who can identify with their own generation. The problem is that many of these people have very limited life experience, are still exploring their own sexuality, are naive regarding personal issues, and even if not intentionally malicious are sometimes absurdly inappropriate and gauche.

Nor should the importance of gender be ignored. While mainline Protestant denominations such as Anglican and United ordain women, have women bishops and leaders, and are increasingly aware of the dangers of patriarchy and sexism, that doesn't always prevent women from being relegated to a lower status than men. This is far more problematic in the Roman Catholic and evangelical churches, with woman denied equality, let alone power and influence. Beyond straightforward sexism, there's a twisted Biblical idea that women are there to serve, and that can lead to all sorts of horrors. For example, Canadian Jean Vanier, founder of L'Arche, a life-changing set of homes for people with intellectual disabilities, convinced his victims that his sexual abuse of them was part of God's plan.

Lastly are those who are abusive by nature and, in the worst cases, intend to use the collar as a means to reach vulnerable people. Grotesque but well-documented. Such abusers, whether they prey on children or adults, can be extremely devious, and some churches are far too trusting. It's an incredibly difficult discernment process for a Christian employer, given the assumption of virtue and necessity for forgiveness integral to the faith, but the safety of congregants has to be paramount. They need to have the same rights and security as students, secular employees, or anybody else.

There are cases going through the Canadian courts right now in which churches are accused of not being sufficiently protective of their members or properly scrutinizing staff. One church administrator to whom I spoke said, "We prayed very hard about whether to hire him. It turns out we were wrong." Let's see how that one goes down with the judge! Sexual abuse is one of the scars of a society that has only recently begun to listen to the stories of the victimized and the assaulted. There's not a place of work or recreation that hasn't been touched, but when it comes to churches, the opportunities for wrong doing are particularly obvious and the consequences horribly damaging.

August 22

Today is the ninetieth anniversary of the first British shot in the First World War, a conflict in which between fifteen and twenty-two million people died and twenty-three million were wounded. It also led to political and geographical devastation, making further international conflict almost inevitable. So, it seems odd, absurd really, to think of a single shot that started the whole bloody thing. While an allied soldier, Alhaji Grunshi of the Gold Coast Regiment, had fired against a German-led force in Togoland on August 7, and an Australian costal artillery battery had opened fire on a German vessel attempting to escape Melbourne on August 5, it was Ernest Edward Thomas, a cavalryman and drummer serving with the 4th Royal Irish Dragoon Guards who fired the first bullet by a British soldier in Europe. It was around 7:00 a.m. this day in 1914, just outside Mons. The war in Europe, fought on the slaughterhouse battlefields of France and Belgium, would lead to a carnage unparalleled in world history.

Born in London of Irish ancestry, Thomas was a corporal in 1914, promoted to sergeant a year later, and joined the machine gun corps a year after that. On one occasion, after entering a German trench and realizing the quality of the German soldiers' boots, he took several pairs, tied them together, and crawled back to his own trench to give them to his comrades. He survived the war and was eventually discharged from the army in 1923, becoming the commissionaire at the Duke of York's Picture House in Brighton. When he died of pneumonia in early 1939, he was buried with full military honours. He was only fifty-four years old but had still survived most of his friends by more than twenty years. A few months after his death, Britain would once again be at war with Germany, in which a further thirty-eight million people would die.

September

September 14

I visit Britain every year, but this trip is a little different. I'm here to attend the opening night of a play at London's Royal Court theatre, and I'm sort of in it. The play is about children's author Roald Dahl and his appalling antisemitism. It's called *Giant*, stars John Lithgow as Dahl, and is written by Mark Rosenblatt. It's set in 1983, the year the author of *Matilda*, *Charlie and the Chocolate Factory*, *The Witches*, *Fantastic Mr. Fox*, and so many other timeless classics gave an interview with *The New Statesman*. During that interview he said, "There is a trait in the Jewish character that does provoke animosity, maybe it's a kind of lack of generosity towards non-Jews," and "I mean, there's always a reason why anti-anything crops up anywhere. Even a stinker like Hitler didn't just pick on them for no reason." I know he said all this because I was the journalist who interviewed him.

I was twenty-four years old and had just started working for *The New Statesman*. I felt rather out of my depth a lot of the time and was surprised and slightly anxious when the editor gave me the job of interviewing Dahl, a man I'd grown up reading and revering. The reason for the interview was that Dahl had just reviewed a book called *God Cried*, an account of Israel's invasion of Lebanon in 1982, for *The Literary Review* magazine. He'd stunned readers with how severe he was, and how his condemnation of Israel seemed to go much further than criticism of a nation-state. He wrote of "a race of people" who had "switched so rapidly from victims to barbarous murderers." He also wrote that the United States was "so utterly dominated by the great Jewish financial institutions" that "they dare not defy" Israel.

When I telephoned him, I genuinely expected him to perhaps apologize for some of what he'd written or at least qualify the harshness and inaccurate generalizations. In fact, the opposite happened. He was polite, not unfriendly, and spoke slowly and deliberately. But it was as though I'd opened the doors on some dark, deep hatred that had been waiting for years to be expressed.

He spoke about the "trait in the Jewish character that does provoke animosity." I wasn't sure I'd heard him correctly, so I stopped him and asked him if he'd meant what he'd said. Could I have possibly misheard him? No, he said, I'd got it right. No remorse, no embarrassment. I told him that three of my grandparents were Jewish. I was sure, anyway, that a man of his intelligence and worldliness would have known that Coren might be a Jewish name. I've never forgotten his reaction. Because there wasn't one. He paused, had clearly heard what I had said, and then calmly continued with his diatribe as though nothing had happened.

He then told me that he'd fought in the Second World War and that he and his friends never saw any Jewish soldiers. I responded again. I told him that my grandfather had spent four years on the front lines in North Africa, Sicily, and Italy, been frequently promoted, and won numerous medals. I explained that hundreds of thousands of Jewish men had been in the British, U.S., Soviet, and other allied armies and if anything, were over-represented in combat roles and heroic deeds. This time I could hear him mumbling something, either to himself or someone else who was in the room. He replied to me as though halfway through a sentence; all I heard was "sticking together." I asked him if there was anything else that he wanted to say. Once again, he was disarmingly courteous. "No, thank you, I think I've made myself very clear. Goodbye." And that was it.

When the call ended, I felt oddly numb and confused. I think I may have been trembling. How could a man who wrote with such genius, such empathy for the downtrodden, and such care for the difference between right and wrong be so vile and arrogant in his racism and so indifferent and cruel toward me? Friends wondered if Dahl was going through some sort of breakdown or crisis, and one of them said, "Oh, I'm sure he didn't mean it." A quite incredible reaction to his repeated and obviously considered remarks. Many years later he would tell another interviewer, "I'm certainly anti-Israeli, and I've become antisemitic ... It's the same old thing: we all know about Jews and the rest of it. There aren't any non-Jewish publishers anywhere, they control the media — jolly clever thing to do — that's why the president of the United States has to sell all this stuff to Israel."

I spoke about it to my late father, who had grown up in a rough part of London in the 1930s and experienced direct antisemitism. "I'm afraid it never disappears but if you let it control you then you let them win. Don't let them bloody win!"

I didn't. I wrote my article repeating what he'd said. He didn't respond himself, but the general reaction surprised me. This was a time before social media and online hysteria, yet there was still a fair amount of outrage at Dahl's statements. But then there were also others who either said that I shouldn't have written the article or even supported what he'd said.

I decided to telephone him again, but he wasn't willing to speak to me. I wrote to him then, asking if there was anything that he'd like to say to me. I suppose I still wanted to make it go away. He replied with the shortest letter I'd ever received. All it said was "No." It was unsigned. Perhaps he thought I'd sell his autograph.

In the following years his fame would increase, and since his death in 1990 his books have been turned into movies year after year. In 2021 Netflix bought Dahl's entire catalogue for around £370 million, and earlier this year we released *Wonka*, the origin story of his 1964 book *Charlie and the Chocolate Factory*. The man's works seem to grow ever more popular. Can the author and his writing be separated? That's something I struggled with in 1983 and still struggle with today. My wife and I read Dahl's stories to our four children, and I'm sure they will to theirs. I'm no fan of cancel culture and I'd never want his books to be removed. But I would like people to be more sensitive to those, like me, who are deeply hurt by someone who hates us just for being who we are and is happy to spew lies and racism without any fear of consequences.

The story has come to the surface every so often. Three years ago, theatre director Mark Rosenblatt asked if he could interview me about what happened. Mark and I met in London, and last year he sent me the script of a play he'd written, insisting quite rightly that I keep the text private. A month or so later he called to say that the Royal Court had agreed to stage it and that the enormously admired and respected movie and stage actor, Tony and Golden Globe winner John Lithgow was to play Dahl. The cast also included Olivier Award winner Elliot Levey, the excellent Rachael Stirling, and Richard Hope, who played my voice on the telephone in the ten-minute conversation that concludes the play. Richard wrote me a few weeks ago to tell me he was playing my voice, but nothing had properly prepared me for actually seeing the play. I attended it with my cousin Giles, a well-known writer, author, and columnist for *The Times*. When we picked up our tickets, the person at the box office said, "Oh, the Michael Coren in the play." I think I mumbled some sort of reply.

The play itself is subtle, balanced, and provocative. The latter because it forces one to think beyond what our comfort zones. Dahl is obviously a difficult man but there's also a compassionate, caring side to him. Some of what he says about Israel and Palestine makes sense, but then he slides over into racism again and again. We're not sure where we stand, who we should listen to, or how to react. Then comes me, and Dahl's antisemitism is obvious and repugnant. As soon as my name was mentioned and then my voice heard, part of me wanted to disappear into the floor. But Giles gave me a very public high five. I was outed.

But who am I kidding? I loved it and wanted to punch my fist into the air and shout, "Yep, that's me." Richard Hope sounded strangely like me, and when I asked him later how that was the case, he said he'd been watching video recordings of me.

Then I attended the first-night party in a world where full clerical dress isn't particularly common. But Mark, the playwright, had told the cast that I was going to be there and that it was likely "he'd be dressed as a priest." Which is why John Lithgow approached me and said, "You're Mike Coren." I replied, "No, I'm supposed to say that 'you're John Lithgow' and then ask for a selfie." I was deeply touched by what he said to me as soon as we met. "Did we get it right, did we do it properly?" The other actors asked me the same thing and revealed a vulnerability and a commitment that moved me deeply. And yes, I did take a bunch of selfies.

The reviews began to appear within hours and continued for the following week. I've seldom seen such unanimously glowing comments about a new play. Cousin Giles wrote in *The Times*, "Best of all for me, was sitting next to one of the real-life characters in the play while an actor spoke his words on stage. This real-time drama culminates in Dahl's famous rant to a young Jewish journalist in 1983. And that journalist was none other than my cousin Mike Coren, still a journalist but now a Canadian and a vicar (it's complicated), who had invited me along as his guest. I know what you're going to say: Wait, what? There's a Coren who is a journalist?"

You see, Giles's dad was the magazine editor and television personality Alan Coren, and his sister is Victoria, who is a bit of a national treasure in Britain what with her writing and broadcasting. I'm flattered to share the name.

This sudden profile had some consequences. I already write fairly regularly for a number of U.K. newspapers and magazines, but I was suddenly asked to write for more. In addition, I had people writing to me as a priest, curious about why I'd been ordained or sometimes wanting spiritual advice. I've a network of clergy friends in Britain and I referred these people to their churches and provided them with contact details.

Transatlantic counselling can be a challenge. It's also a challenge for me to decide where I'm happiest and where I truly belong. I came to Canada in 1987 to marry a Canadian, we raised four children here, and the country has been extremely good to me. But as I age, I miss what formed me in the early years, and I doubt that this is an emotion confined to me. Some of that experience can never be rediscovered because people have gone, things have changed. But not the medieval architecture, the smells of the morning, the Victorian streets, the Essex forests, and the friendships that were formed in my first twenty-eight years.

September 18

Tea with my friend Richard Coles, who is the only Anglican priest I know of to have had a number one single in the pop charts. He was in The Communards, and their song "Don't Leave Me This Way" is still played today. I got to know Richard when I was considering becoming an Anglican and I value him more than I can say. As well as writing memoirs and detective stories, he also wrote a book about the death of his partner. He's a man who has chronicled his own tempestuous journey, witnessed many of his friends succumb to AIDS, had personal encounters with depression, and is a skilled observer and commentator. So it's no surprise that he has recorded the events of his husband's death and the first year of his own agony so memorably. The book is called *The Madness of Grief*, and I highly recommend it.

"I felt like a war correspondent, even though I've never been one, with bombs going off and windows smashing," he told me. "I simply tried to record all of that as accurately as I could. The book wasn't cathartic, not at all, and many people advised me not to write it. I understand what they meant, because it's not until the second year that you realize he's not coming back. I was in the early stages, they said, and this was long-term, it was forever."

September 29

I started watching the Tottenham football team sixty years ago when my dad took me, and old habits die hard. I was born four miles from the stadium and have followed them all of my life. They're playing Manchester United today in Manchester, so I go the closest pub in Westminster, where I stay when I'm in London, to watch the game. I order a pint of beer, take a seat, and wait for the game to start. It's crowded and loud and then I see people look round at me. It's the clerical collar again. They're drinking, they're passionate, they're going to shout and swear, and they're wondering if such behaviour is appropriate with a priest sitting there. I really didn't even remember I was wearing the collar. I drink deep, put my glass down, and then say, "Dad was a Jewish cabbie from Hackney,

I bleed blue and white, I'm not taking my collar off, and bollocks to Man United." There's a brief silence and then a loud cheer, and lots of people offer to buy me a drink. I must do this more often. And we win 3–0!

It's funny but significant. There can be a degree of preciosity with some clergy, too great an emphasis on the trappings of the church, and a fear of that glorious ordinariness that's so often mocked by those who regard themselves as learned and thoughtful. I've spoken to several Theology on Tap groups, where gatherings of Christians meet in a pub to discuss religious issues, and that's fun and productive. But being in the middle of a collection of working-class people, roaring for your team, and being unwaveringly partisan can break down all sorts of barriers.

October

October 7

I've a new book published. It's my twentieth, and while the thrill and novelty of holding a new book never disappears, the euphoria does diminish over the years. This time's a little different, however. After decades of writing books about other people, mostly those long dead, I've now written about myself, not yet dead. What a curious, slightly disturbing feeling it is. Not that it's my final book, since I just signed a contract for another one, but it's in some ways a last word on my life and that calls for sobering reflection.

The title is *Heaping Coals: From Media Firebrand to Anglican Priest*. One of the central themes, perhaps the most central of the book, is the journey toward ordination. It is, I suppose, a spiritual autobiography. Paradoxically, becoming a priest wasn't even a remote possibility for most of my life, but as I wrote the book I realized how if I looked behind the curtain, there was that emerging pattern of something almost inevitable. Where would I find meaning, what am I about, what is it that genuinely matters?

But oh, what a circuitous route. A secular, half-Jewish, working-class family and upbringing, clever but lazy, a fully funded university education, drugs, parties, and irresponsibility, and then a career in journalism, arrived at partly because I'd no idea what else to do. Working with Oscar-winning screenwriters, hanging out with Salman Rushdie and Martin Amis, writing books with famous broadcasters, appearing on radio and television, being published by one of the most respected companies in Britain.

All this by my mid-twenties. And the emerging realization that I was no happier than I'd been before. That stung, that made me think, that pushed me toward faith. Then meeting and falling in love with a Canadian, emigrating, and twenty years of radio, television, books, and column-writing, often on the conservative side of politics.

Then a conversion to a faith I'd never known before, something deep and progressive and fulfilling and challenging. That conversion, that slide into ordination, came at a serious cost, both professional and personal, but it released my soul, revealed the inner workings, made me the Christian I always wanted to be. It was cathartic and liberating but it was also painful and disturbing. Being forced to ask questions about my own life, and my own being. To be critical and honest.

I knew that I'd said and written things over the years that demanded redress and contrition, and for more than a decade have done all in my power to repair and reform. But as I reflected on my life, I thought about how I'd treated those people who loved me and cared for me. I found myself sitting at my desk before dawn — I've an eccentric writing schedule — close to tears, even openly weeping, about my behaviour. Some of the people I think I hurt are gone now and I can't call or write or apologize to them. That's what prayer is for, that's what self-reflection is for. We've all made mistakes; none of us are perfect. Yet I'm still on that path of self-forgiveness and not sure if I'll ever reach the end. Not entirely sure I'm supposed to.

The solace I find is in Christ. There, I've said it. In Him, in him alone. Does that make me sound rather evangelical? If so, I rejoice in it. The longer I spend as a priest, the more I realize that. What gets me through, what makes it all possible, is the word made flesh, the Son of God. Sixty-five years of life, recorded in an autobiography, given a central thread by being a follower of Christ and being ordained as a priest. I'm so glad that I wrote this book but just as happy that I won't have to do it again.

It's been well received — or at least those people who don't like it don't tell me so.

Apart from one, who writes a zero-star review on Amazon. I'm pretty sure it's the same person who gave the same verdict on my last book. Call me a cynic if you like, but I've a sneaking feeling that he doesn't actually read them. That was certainly the case with one of the books because he wrote the review before the thing was even published. Most of the other Amazon comments are five-star so the average works out, but I do wonder if these even count for anything.

I'm given lovely interviews on CBC radio and on TV by TV Ontario, where Steve Paikin — a friend for thirty-five years — began the show thus: "Has there ever been a more intriguing personal journey by a Canadian journalist than Michael Coren's? Once a conservative provocateur. Actually, no, let's call him what he often was. A pain in the ass." It was one of the finest interviews I've ever had.

There were also a number of podcasts, some with sizeable followings, and a fairly long interview on a large radio station, during which I soon realized that the interviewer had no idea why I was there. Had he read the book? No. Did he know the book's title? No. Oh well, it's all publicity in the end.

October 12

A very touching moment during a wedding I'm taking. Bride and groom are very nervous, and their guests are demonstrative, perhaps rowdy at times. We have a rule against throwing confetti because it takes an age to clear up. Turn off your phones, don't throw confetti, but everybody is welcome. One little girl has a basket of petals, and while she wasn't formally handing them out to people, they were going all over the church. The ceremony ended, everybody went outside for the official photos, and we set about cleaning the dismantled flower parts. Suddenly the bride appeared, obviously embarrassed, and asked if she could do the cleaning for us because she said it was her fault. I thank her but tell her to get out, enjoy her wedding day, and have a marvelous life.

October 15

I attend a lecture about the Community of the Cross of Nails, which on first hearing doesn't sound like a fun evening. It's based around the bombing of Coventry during the Second World War and the subject had always fascinated me. In my early twenties, I'd go to see Shakespearean plays at Stratford in the English midlands. I didn't have very much money so would cycle to Euston Station in London, put my bike on the train, go to Coventry, and then cycle to Stratford. I'd usually sleep rough on the edge of the forest, then cycle back to Coventry, and repeat the journey in reverse. Romantic I suppose, but to think of it now in my mid-sixties is terrifying. The energy and effort, the dedication to theatre, and the love of Jacobean drama. The last, at least, has stayed with me all of my life. Because of all this I got to know Coventry, and the damage caused by the bombing was obvious even in the early 1990s.

It was November 14 and 15, 1940, when the Luftwaffe carried out one of the most effective bombing raids of the entire war. Coventry was a major manufacturing centre and was based around a beautiful, medieval core that was highly flammable.

Thirty-thousand incendiary and 503 tons of high-explosive bombs were used, killing 568 people and seriously injuring a further 850. The centre of the city was smashed and the fourteenth-century Gothic cathedral destroyed. The city was unprepared, and while the British had radar and could see the German force flying over the coast, they had no idea where the bombers were headed. A conspiracy theory has developed over the years that Prime Minister Winston Churchill knew about the raid through Britain's secret code interception machines but was unable to intervene because it would have indicated to the Germans that their codes could be broken. It's utter nonsense.

One woman who was there when the bombing took place said that she "saw a dog running down the street with a child's arm in its mouth." There was panic and hysteria. Bodies were laid out with luggage tags tied to them so that they could be identified, but a second bombing wave blew the roof off the temporary mortuary, the rain came in, the tags became damp, the ink ran, and many of the bodies could no longer be identified. It was, said one witness, "the closest I thought I'd ever see to what hell must be like."

From this horror came the community I've come to hear about. Spread across the world are 260 churches, chaplaincies, retreat centres, and schools dedicated to the three central principles of healing the wounds of history, learning to live with difference and diversity, and building a culture of peace and justice. It's most active in Germany, Britain, and the U.S. but has affiliates across Europe and in Africa. The talk is inspiring, but I was brought up on war movies, toy soldiers, and a suspicion and even dislike of the Germans — it was only twenty years after the end of the war. Yet my grandpa, who went through four years of the conflict in North Africa and Italy, didn't seem to hold any hatred. He positively loved Italy and Italians. So, my difficulty with forgiveness just won't do.

Corrie ten Boom was a Dutch Christian living under Nazi rule, and she, her father, and her sister had been arrested and put into a concentration camp. Her father and sister didn't survive. After the war she preached understanding and forgiveness. One night after a church service in Munich, she saw in the congregation the former SS soldier who had guarded part of the processing centre at Ravensbrück concentration camp, where she and her family had been incarcerated. The horrors came back to her, and then this man approached, bowing and smiling, and said how much he's appreciated her words, and how he now knew that Christ had washed his sins away. "His hand was thrust out to shake mine," she said. "And I, who had preached so often to the people the need to forgive, kept my hand at my side. Even as the angry, vengeful thoughts boiled through me, I saw the sin of them. Jesus Christ had died for this man; was I going to ask for more? Lord Jesus, I prayed, forgive me and help me to forgive him. I tried to smile; I struggled to raise my hand. I could not. I felt nothing, not the slightest spark of warmth or charity. And so again I breathed a silent prayer. Jesus, I cannot forgive him. Give me Your Forgiveness. As I took his hand the most incredible thing happened. From my shoulder along my arm and through my hand a current seemed to pass from me to him, while into my heart sprang a love for this stranger that almost overwhelmed me."

How dare I not forgive?

There's a wonderful translation of the Bible by a man called Eugene Peterson called *The Message*, and he translates one passage like this: "You'll even be turned in by parents, brothers, relatives, and friends. Some of you will be killed. There's no telling who will hate you because of me. Even so, every detail of your body and soul — even the hairs of your head! — is in my care; nothing of you will be lost. Staying with it — that's what is required. Stay with it to the end. You won't be sorry; you'll be saved."

October 19

Toronto's Yonge-Dundas Square is disappointing. It's supposed to be the heart of the largest city in Canada but it's architecturally bland and culturally lacking. Still, as a meeting-place and a reference point it does the job. But not for much longer under its present name, because the city council has voted to remove the reference to Dundas and rename the place Sankofa Square, from the Twi language in Ghana that means "to go back and get it."

There are Dundas streets all over Ontario and even a town with the name because Henry Dundas, Viscount Melville, a close ally of Prime Minister Pitt the Younger, was closely connected to the foundation of modern Canada. But supporters of the name change insist that he was also insufficiently opposed to the slave trade. In other words, he was a racist.

But that's not strictly true. Dundas was an abolitionist who spoke out against the evils of slavery, but unlike William Wilberforce and his group, he advocated a more gradual and arguably more practical approach to achieving the same end. It's not clear-cut by any means. Ironically, the Akan people in Ghana, the people who spoke Twi, were active participants in slavery, and sold African men, women, and children to Europeans slavers. But as we've seen throughout the debate about renaming, removing, and cancelling, historical accuracy isn't always the motivating factor. Some of those thrown into the dustbin of history obviously deserve it, but is there room for nuance, and are we being consistent and fair?

Toronto saw this two years ago when Ryerson University, once an urban polytechnic, was rebranded as Toronto Metropolitan University. The reason was that the eponymous Egerton Ryerson, a nineteenth-century religious leader and education reformer, was allegedly a supporter of the notorious residential school system that — even if not always intended to do so — broke up families and led to enormous pain and suffering. That system only officially ended in 1996, and the trauma is felt to this day. The treatment of First Nations people, both historically and currently, is quite rightly an acute issue, but while Ryerson was certainly far from innocent in all this, he was also a progressive thinker and activist who campaigned for universal education, and believed that poverty should never be an obstacle to learning. He lived with the Credit Ojibwe people for a year, learned their language, and was given an Ojibwe name. Yet the physical attacks on his statue and the campaign against his name, achievements, and reputation didn't take very much of all this into account. The same is now applied to Henry Dundas, as it has been to a whole regiment of Canadian politicians and public figures who had the audacity to live in a less politically correct age.

The Dundas example is in some way even more jarring, because nobody seems to know where the initiative began. Polls reveal that the vast majority of Torontonians are against the move, a petition of thirty thousand signatures in opposition achieved nothing, and the cost of the change will be in the hundreds of thousands of dollars. This at a time when homelessness, public transport decay, and drug problems in the city have become more severe, and essential services are crying out for increased funding. They'll have to get in line because one of Toronto's relatively few tourist attractions, Black Creek Pioneer Village, a recreation of settler life in colonial Canada, is to be renamed The Village at Black Creek, which makes it sound like some sort of shopping and spa location. The people at the living museum have said that "for too long the site focused on settlers of European descent, the Village has been working to change the narrative by collaborating with Indigenous scholars, artists, elders, and community members since 2017." This too comes at a financial cost.

But none of this should come as a particular surprise. Last year the Girl Guides of Canada renamed the Brownies the

Embers because the word "brownie" was considered too racially divisive and, according to Girl Guide leaders, "caused harm and was a barrier to belonging for racialised girls and women." That came as a surprise to my mixed-race daughters, who were once enthusiastic Brownies.

October 24

It's the centenary of the infamous Zinoviev Letter, which is not something that will lead to parties and celebrations, at least not in normal homes. In 1924 in Britain, the Labour Party had formed its first government. It was a minority administration, dependent on the Liberals, and was under siege from its formation. While party leader and Prime Minister Ramsay MacDonald was moderate, pragmatic, and certainly anti-Communist, he and his party were constantly accused of being overly sympathetic to Moscow. Their decision to normalize Britain's relationship with the Soviets, only seven years after the Russian Revolution, fuelled paranoia about "Bolshevik influence," and this fear extended to some within the security services. It was partly the notion that Labour was too close to the Soviets that led to the MacDonald government losing a confidence vote and having to call an election.

Four days before the election, the *Daily Mail* published a letter ostensibly from Grigori Zinoviev, head of the Communist International in Moscow, the dreaded Comintern. It ordered the Communist Party of Great Britain to commit acts of sedition and argued that "a settlement of relations between the two countries will assist in the revolutionising of the international and British proletariat not less than a successful rising in any of the working districts of England, as the establishment of close contact between the British and Russian proletariat, the exchange of delegations and workers, etc., will make it possible for us to extend and develop the propaganda of ideas of Leninism in England and the Colonies."

It sounds like a parody today but at the time was taken seriously, even by some who claimed to be experts. The Soviets were in fact anxious to build closer ties with Britain, but less due to ideology than to Russia's poverty and desperate need for loans and financial support. As a result, Zinoviev himself quickly denied that the letter was genuine. But as anti-Communists said at the time: well, he would say that, wouldn't he?

Although Labour leaders were furious, their eventual vote wasn't especially damaged by the letter, with supporters either not believing its authenticity or not caring even if was true. The party also ran more candidates than before, so the overall vote tally was higher. The Conservatives were always strong favourites to win but certainly attracted voters who were genuinely frightened of what would happen if a Labour government formed closer ties with Moscow. The major victim of the letter was probably the Liberal Party, already in a rapid decline. These "red scare" tactics pushed many of their usual voters into the hands of the Conservatives.

But it also led to a lasting Labour Party suspicion of British as well as Soviet Communism, and a determination to emphasize the non-Marxist nature of British social democracy, something that was only interrupted when Jeremy Corbyn became leader. We see this in Canada too with the NDP. Partly as a result of the letter, the new Prime Minister Stanley Baldwin distanced his government from Moscow, and the Soviet Union became increasingly isolated.

That would have delighted the writers of the letter, who were almost certainly white Russians, monarchists, or other émigrés who wanted to discredit the Labour Party and prevent Britain from aiding the Soviets in any way. The Zinoviev Letter was a hoax, and that so many people believed and continued to believe its authenticity says more about popular paranoia than about the authenticity of the letter. Within a few years, Stalin controlled the Soviet Union, incarcerated and killed millions, and oversaw a forced starvation of Ukraine. Courageous people wrote genuine letters about what was going on inside the country, but their letters were usually given far less acceptance than the Zinoviev forgery.

As for Ramsay MacDonald, he would go on to be Labour Prime Minister once again between 1929 and 1931 and then lead a national government until 1935. In 1934 Grigory Zinoviev was arrested, put on trial in Moscow, and accused of crimes against the Soviet Union. The following year, after torture and humiliation, he was ordered to plead guilty to various false charges. He said he would do so if his life was spared. "That," said Stalin, "goes without saying." He was then executed.

November

November 2

This week I presided over a baptism in the morning and a funeral in the afternoon. That was a first for me and it may well be the only time this ever happens in my clerical career. Such polarized events, such extremes of emotion. The hopes and aspirations of loving parents, the pain and loneliness of grieving children and partners. The living, breathing narrative of our existence, in all of its fragility and beauty. The precious borders of our lives should open us up revealing intimacy and vulnerability, leading us to question our actions and filter our emotions and feelings through a prism of goodness and kindness. The experience of such significant events, whether baptisms, weddings, or funerals, becomes a catalyst on our self-awareness.

People of faith have prayer at the centre of our lives, and in that act of prayer we should let go, allow, and accept. In a way, it's a profound acquiescence or perhaps a reluctant acceptance that we may not know what is best, and that there is someone above and beyond us. Then comes the superb paradox for those of us who are Christian: that in defeat is victory, and in death is life. It's so bitingly contrary to a world that increasingly celebrates wealth, power, and prestige, no matter what the cost.

For me, both baptisms and funerals sing tunes of selflessness, the abandonment of the ego, and the gorgeous acknowledgement that we're all — religious or not — part of a physical and a spiritual collective. Take it slowly, take in gradually. None of this is completely transparent or even obvious, but then God seldom does the transparent or the obvious. What the Almighty does do is remind us that we can be better and do better, and that in our smiles of welcome and tears of farewell we can help to make the world the place it could, and ought to, be.

What should form us isn't the stock market but the market of generosity and care; not the speeches of politicians but the sacrifices of ordinary people; not the empty narcissism of reality television and show business flamboyance but the full and gritty grace of those who anonymously perform the thousand small miracles that keep optimism alive. We have merely a few decades on earth to make a difference, and it doesn't have to be one that is recorded in history books or makes the news. I've met too many genuine saints, largely unknown beyond their family and community, to believe otherwise.

November 5

Guy Fawkes Night, the day in Britain where they celebrate the fact that Guy Fawkes and his friends failed to blow up Parliament and murder the king and his family, the government, almost the entire British establishment, and countless ordinary people who lived and worked in the area. The Gunpowder Plot in 1605 was the work of a bunch of Roman Catholic extremists who in fact made life far worse for British Catholics and were condemned by most of their co-religionists.

Catholics were certainly treated badly at the time, but there were also many wealthy, powerful, and government-supporting Catholics, some of whom would have died if the plot had been successful. Fawkes, Thomas and Robert Winter, Robert Catesby, John and Christopher Wright, Thomas Percy, and the rest were violent fanatics with views that today would be considered horribly reactionary and intolerant, and it's always amused me that far-left demonstrators often wear Guy Fawkes masks during their demonstrations.

Guy Fawkes was one of my favourite times of the year when I was a child, and I didn't know anybody who regarded it as anti-Catholic or political in any way. It was a time to watch fireworks, eat hotdogs, and have fun.

November 8

Lunch with a dear friend who was once a newspaper editor but is now a prominent figure in the climate justice movement. The number of people I know who began in media, did very well, but now work elsewhere is a bad sign for a healthy media and democracy. My friend is a mum, and a wonderful one, and inevitably we discuss family, and I mention my lovely German son-in-law, the father of our grandchild. I tell a joke about the German national character. A British couple adopt Wolfgang, a German baby. He's well and healthy but doesn't speak. One year, two years, and finally approaching his third birthday there's been not a word. Mum and dad are worried and prepare to take their son to the doctor. Then, one day, they give him a plate of apple strudel. Suddenly he says, "This strudel is tepid." Amazed and delighted, they hug their son and ask why he's never said a word until this moment. He replies, "Because up to now everything has generally been acceptable." I must ask my son-in-law if this joke is acceptable.

November 10

It's the birthday of Martin Luther. It was in 1483 but he's still a powerfully influential figure, and there are churches and even denominations named after him. While dissent within Christendom began before Luther, he was the great catalyst, the German monk and professor who nailed his *Ninety-Five Theses* on the door of the castle church in Wittenberg, thus lighting the fuse that blew the Roman Catholic Church apart. It matters far more than one might think, because it was not only religion but politics, culture, and economics that would change in that hammering's wake. In the document, Luther made public his condemnation of the sale of indulgences — money paid by friends and relatives to reduce the time spent by the dead in purgatory, a sort of waiting room before heaven. But this academic disputation went much further than that. History was given a reboot.

There's much that is positive about Luther. He liberated people from rigid church control, gave impeccable energy to the idea of the individual's relationship with God, and worked to eliminate corruption and superstition. In many ways, he was a pioneer not just of religious change, but of modernity itself. But behind his undeniable genius was a gritty nastiness. He could be crude, abusive, angry, and, perhaps most tragically, deeply antisemitic — a legacy that needs to be grappled with even 500 years later. He started as a supporter of the Jewish people, arguing quite rightly that they had been badly treated by the Roman Catholic Church, and quite wrongly that they, if presented with what he regarded as a more authentic Christianity, would surely convert. In 1523 he wrote an essay, entitled "That Jesus Was Born a Jew," condemning the fact that the church had "dealt with the Jews as if they were dogs rather than human beings; they have done little else than deride them and seize their property."

But the Jews did not convert, and Luther reacted appallingly. In 1543, he published "The Jews and Their Lies," which today is shocking in its venom, and even for its time stood out as particularly cruel and intolerant. In the sixty-five-thousand-word treatise, he calls for a litany of horrors including the destruction of synagogues, Jewish schools, and homes; for rabbis to be forbidden to preach; for the stripping of legal protection of Jews on highways; for the confiscation of their money. The Jews are, wrote Luther, a "base, whoring people, that is, no people of God, and their boast of lineage, circumcision, and law must be accounted as filth."

Some of his defenders have claimed that Luther was old and ill when he wrote this, ignoring the fact that he lived another three years after the essay and that most of us become mildly grumpy when we feel unwell, not genocidal. Plus, Luther had also managed to have the Jews expelled from Saxony and some German towns as early as 1537.

His sway over the German church lived on. Martin Sasse was the bishop of the Evangelical Church of Thuringia during Kristallnacht in 1938. He feted the pogroms and the mass destruction of synagogues and Jewish businesses, and even tied it explicitly to Luther himself; just days after what was in effect the beginning of the organized slaughter of the Jews, he distributed a pamphlet entitled "Martin Luther on the Jews: Away with Them!" in which he claimed the Nazis were acting as Christians in their violent antisemitism, and that this was precisely what Luther would have wanted.

Yet there was also a powerful anti-Nazi movement within Lutheranism, and the sacrifice and martyrdom of those pastors and laypeople must never be forgotten. The Confessing Church was formed in opposition to the regime's attempt to unify all German Protestants into a single pro-Nazi church. Leaders like Martin Niemöller and Heinrich Grüber were sent to concentration camps but survived; writer and activist Dietrich Bonhoeffer, who was accused of being part of a plot to assassinate Adolf Hitler, did not survive. His writings have influenced countless people and still influence me. I number him as a hero. “Nothing that we despise in other men is inherently absent from ourselves. We must learn to regard people less in the light of what they do or don’t do, and more in light of what they suffer.” His 1937 book *The Cost of Discipleship* is still essential reading. “Judging others makes us blind, whereas love is illuminating. By judging others, we blind ourselves to our own evil and to the grace which others are just as entitled to as we are.” And “Cheap grace is the grace we bestow on ourselves. Cheap grace is the preaching of forgiveness without requiring repentance, baptism without church discipline, Communion without confession ... Cheap grace is grace without discipleship, grace without the cross, grace without Jesus Christ, living and incarnate.”

In 1994, the five-million-member Evangelical Lutheran Church in America spoke publicly of Luther’s “anti-Judaic diatribes” and denounced “the violent recommendations of his later writings against the Jews.” The Central Council of Jews in Germany had long asked for a formal statement from Lutherans on the subject of antisemitism, and just last year, the Lutheran Church in Germany obliged, condemning Luther’s writings on the Jews and “the part played by the Reformation tradition in the painful history between Christians and Jews.” The state Lutheran churches in Norway and the Netherlands have followed suit. Other Lutheran churches reacted earlier; the American Lutheran Church, for instance, acknowledged it as early as 1974. In 1998, on the sixtieth anniversary of Kristallnacht, the Evangelical Lutheran Church in Bavaria issued a declaration that “it is imperative for the Lutheran Church, which knows itself to be indebted to the work and tradition of Martin Luther, to take seriously also his anti-Jewish utterances, to acknowledge their theological function, and to reflect on their consequences. It has to distance itself from anti-Judaism in Lutheran theology."

November 17

Many churches hold meetings for Friends of Bill or Friends of Bill W. It's a code, a euphemism, for Alcoholics Anonymous, cofounded in 1935 by William Wilson and Bob Smith. Wilson's legacy is truly memorable, yet while he gave up drinking, didn't drink for the last thirty-six years of his life, and showed others how to do the same, he was a heavy smoker, eventually suffered from emphysema, and smoked even when dependant on an oxygen tank. Such a tragic end to a remarkable life.

A young, well-dressed man parked his expensive car and came to the door of the church and handed me an envelope containing a cheque for quite a large amount of money. I thanked him but also asked why. "I just want to tell you guys how grateful we are for hosting us for so long and helping me to change my life around, to save it really." He smiled and took a breath. "Friend of Bill's, friend of Bill's." Never think for a moment that alcoholics are obvious. I'm constantly surprised by the number of people I meet who are recovering alcoholics.

My parents hardly ever drank, and I wasn't raised in a drinking culture, but in the last few years I've found that a large glass of Talisker, Highland Park, or Glenlivet complete my day. But how large is that glass and how dependant am I on it? I don't think I have a problem, but then I've met too many people who say the same thing and continue to do so even when that problem is wrecking their lives. A friend who has struggled with alcohol for many years said to me recently, "I've been told to never drink alone but drinking when I'm alone is when I enjoy it most. I no longer feel alone, you see."

November 20

I've never had any doubts about my vocation as a priest after I was ordained, but when I was at seminary I did wonder if I'd complete the course. I'm pretty sure that those doubts were about myself rather than what I was aspiring to. I was ordained a deacon in October 2019 and "priested" in September 2021. Being a priest means that we're allowed to consecrate the eucharist and give absolution, but it's little different from being a deacon. For me, the first ordination, as a deacon, was the more dramatic and moving experience. Now I can't imagine being anything other than a priest and can't remember a time when I wasn't ordained and didn't have the privilege of holy orders. There are times when presiding at the Mass, the eucharistic service, when I feel a sense of completion that I can only compare to my wedding day or when I saw our children born. Overwhelmed, unworthy, in awe, and with both a weight of responsibility and a feeling of sublime lightness and freedom.

November 21

Relaxing at home after a long day I watch *Father Brown*, the cozy if anodyne crime television series where a quite shocking number of people are killed in one small village, and a Roman Catholic priest is there to solve every crime. *Father Brown* is based on G.K. Chesterton's novels, but the new TV version has little connection to the original. The author of *The Napoleon of Notting Hill*, *Orthodoxy*, numerous biographies, and volumes of columns was a Christian, and his faith was the essence of his thought and work. It would be absurd to try to understand the man without acknowledging his Roman Catholicism. Yet that's exactly what has happened. Compare the highly successful current television *Father Brown* stories with the Kenneth More series from 1974. Fifty years ago, we had much of the original text, and its pre–Vatican II Catholicism could be challenging, even disturbing. Today the little detective priest is entertaining, fun, and decidedly non-Chestertonian.

A similar process of de-Christianization occurred with the 1993 film *Shadowlands*, adapted from the glorious stage play about C.S. Lewis and his romance with Joy Davidman. Almost all of the references to prayer, heaven, faith, and the divinity of Jesus were expunged from the play's script in the adaptation, leaving the grand knight of Christianity — arguably the most influential Christian apologist in modern times — as a rather caricatured Oxford professor who struggled with emotion until a loud New Yorker entered his life. It may just be entertainment, but it informs the public's perception of Christianity, and it's indicative of a deeper loss — the widespread decline of the Christian public intellectual. There are plenty of highly intelligent Christians around, but for a variety of reasons, they're seldom especially public.

There are exceptions. The author and broadcaster Tom Holland, whom I'm glad to call a friend, was a well-known and respected historian of the ancient world long before he wrote and spoke about Christianity. His book *Dominion* makes the case for the "Christian revolution" and how even when we're not aware of it, our assumptions are formed by and based in the Christian experience. Holland explains his faith thus: "I crave the enchantment. A Christianity that has bled itself of enchantment is a pallid and anaemic thing." This is significant, because what we often encounter in public life are commentators who may be Christian but manage to disguise their belief by what they'd describe as the practicalities of politics and policy. In other words, they play down the deity bit. Remember, for example, Tony Blair's fixer Alastair Campbell allegedly explaining that "We don't do God" when a journalist asked about the former British prime minister's religious faith. It's not helped by commentators whose only interest in Christianity is to ask someone where they stand on LGBTQ2S rights or women's choice.

The author Francis Spufford has managed to avoid all this. He's probably best-known as a novelist whose first book, *Golden Hill*, won the Costa Book Award and Ondaatje Prize, among others, and *Light Perpetual* in 2021 was Booker Prize longlisted. But he also wrote *Unapologetic: Why, Despite Everything, Christianity Can Still Make Surprising Emotional Sense*, perhaps the sharpest, punchiest, and most bitingly erudite defence of Christianity of this generation. He writes, "I don't know if there's a God. (And neither do you, and neither does Professor Dawkins, and neither does anybody. It isn't the kind of thing you can know. It isn't a knowable item.) But then, like every human being, I am not in the habit of entertaining only the emotions I can prove. I'd be an unrecognizable oddity if I did."

Of Christian intellectual life, Spufford told *Premier Christianity* magazine, "People are wary of explicit Christianity because it may be embarrassing, and because they think it may be propaganda. And not being rude, but some of the things that go by the name of Christian art are not very good. Some of the attempts to create parallel worlds of especially Christian music or entertainment seem to settle for a world that's too small." A leading journalist in Toronto told me privately that he attends church, prays, and believes, but keeps it private. "Not because I'd be fired or even attacked, but because my credibility would be questioned. I'd have to first explain that I didn't think the world was literally created in six days, did believe in abortion rights and gay marriage, did think Donald Trump was a terrible advertisement for Christianity." He refused to allow me to name him in this diary, and therein lies the point.

Partly as a response, thinking Christians have too often retreated into the bunker of consensus. Take the number of Christian publishing companies that have developed or expanded in the last twenty years, mostly Catholic and evangelical but mainstream Protestant too. That can lead to a problem of insularity, of authors and thinkers wanting to write to a specifically Christian audience. Where public Christians have been successful is on the harsh Right of the church. Blogs such as *Lifesite News*, with an enormous following, seem to become more right-wing all the time. They began as an anti-abortion platform but now address a whole variety of issues, often with a conservative aggression that would shame mainstream conservative Christians. These extreme media platforms are increasingly numerous and popular, producing their own type of public intellectual, which an emphasis more on the public than the intellectual.

How different all this is from the faith and witness of C.S. Lewis, who rejected a CBE (Commander of the British Empire) in the 1952 honours list because he was reluctant to identify with any political position. He also insisted that being a Christian didn't require that we leave our minds at the cross. "God is no fonder of intellectual slackers than of any other slackers. If you are thinking of becoming a Christian, I warn you, you are embarking on something which is going to take the whole of you, brains and all."

The church would also do well to look within. Archbishop of Canterbury Rowan Williams held the office for almost ten years, retiring in December 2012. He was considered the finest intellectual to lead the English church in many centuries and had erudite opinions on most subjects in public life. His successors were intelligent and educated men but highly limited in comparison. It's not that Williams was the most effective primate but that he was accepted outside of the church as an esteemed thinker. When he spoke, people listened.

Canadian author Jordan Peterson flirts with Christianity and, whatever one thinks of his ideas, he has a major following among young men in particular. But I'd be horrified if he were regarded as a Christian public intellectual, and in some ways the Peterson brand is part of the problem. He can be overly emotional, harshly absolute in his responses, and so verbose as to be downright confusing. But there's no denying that his style is effective, and that poses another problem. If people are eager for sweeping answers without wanting to ask valid and perhaps troubling questions, how can an intelligent Christian faith proper in the public square?

The question is whether any of this really matters. We have more philosophers and commentators of the Left, Right, and most positions in between than we know what to do with. That, however, is precisely why informed, sophisticated, and orthodox Christian voices are more necessary than ever. Two thousand years of theology, witness, and thought may provide an alternative to the polarization that so dominates the public square.

November 22

Schadenfreude, the taking of pleasure in someone else's failure or pain, is one of the most difficult errors — okay, let me call it a sin — to avoid. It is wrong to feel that sense of righteousness or joy in someone's decline, especially if that person is an enemy or has hurt us in some way. I consider this as I learn today of even more legal and career troubles for someone, a priest, who hurt me and lied about me, and did so from a prominent and powerful position.

How should I react? By trying to feel what he's feeling, to see the brokenness, the humanity, to ask if I could have found myself in the same position. I'd never have done precisely what he did but my goodness, I've also done things that appal me, that were selfish and wrong and sometimes worse.

When Jesus asked the accusers of a woman whether they had ever behaved badly, ever lusted over a woman, ever lusted over her for that matter, he was exposing hypocrisy. Are you any better, are you clean, are you qualified to judge other people?

There were three notable deaths on this day, 22 November, in 1963. President Kennedy was assassinated, and *Brave New World* author Aldous Huxley and C.S. Lewis also died. My dear friend Walter Hooper knew Lewis, and I miss kind, humble, clever Walter all the time. He entered a nursing home for the last weeks of his life and fell victim to the dark devil of Covid-19.

I was a child when Lewis died, which is why I was so fortunate to become friends with Walter, Lewis's last secretary, and as such one of the final conduits for the author of the Narnia stories, *Mere Christianity*, *The Screwtape Letters*, and so many more. I always remember the last time I saw Walter in Oxford, England. He said he had a gift for me, a book. I asked him to sign it, but he said almost apologetically, "Michael, I can no longer write." I asked him what he meant. "I can no longer hold the pen." My heart broke. The gift he had used for more than five decades, the written word, was now denied him.

He was born in North Carolina in 1931, studied in Britain, and had written to Lewis as an admirer. Lewis replied, the two developed a friendship, and Walter became his private secretary. After Lewis's death in 1963, Walter went on to become a literary adviser to his estate, an editor of Lewis's letters and papers, and a frequent speaker at conferences on the legacy of perhaps the finest communicator of the Christian message in modern times. Walter also knew J.R.R. Tolkien, who lived until 1973, and spoke and wrote of the friendship between Lewis and the author of *The Lord of the Rings*. Every time I went to see him, I'd ask for more anecdotes, like some glutton never full, and he wouldn't refuse. He once said to me, "I know that when people visit me from America, Australia, Japan, anywhere, what they really want to know is what was Lewis like." A pause. "And that's OK, that's OK." In other words, he was aware that he was a point of contact for one long gone, and sought after for someone else. But his invincible humility allowed that to flourish, and he embraced it as vocation.

I'll always remember his delight when playing with our children, and I can't help thinking it was partly because they had no motive other than fun, and they were with "Mr. Hooper" rather than a friend of someone else.

We spoke of Lewis's fondness for beer and tea, his teasing of Walter over his use of American English, the decline he experienced after the death of his wife, Joy, his indifference to worldly success, and of course his faith. "Not sure what he'd think of some of these modern Christians," said Walter once over an evening meal at the Trout Inn in Oxford. "They sometimes quote him but I'm not sure if they understand him." Then there was the story of Lewis attending his nearby Anglican church. He would always leave just as the final words were spoken, eager to avoid others. On one occasion he got to the old, heavy door to find it accidentally locked, and made such a noise trying to open it that the entire congregation turned in silence to look at him. "He was red-faced most of the time," said Walter, "but that day shades of purple began to emerge."

Walter made the world a better place, influenced countless people, and helped keep alight the flame of a man he revered. There will be no more journeys to that beautiful apartment in Woodstock Close, no more pub lunches, no more sparkling smiles as another story was told. I'll pray for him but most of all I'll thank him, and I know I'll be one of many.

November 25

I see an advance screening of a new movie, *Bonhoeffer: Pastor Spy Assassin*. It's an imperfect account of the life of Dietrich Bonhoeffer, the German Lutheran pastor and anti-Nazi dissident who was a founding member of the Confessing Church, the Christian alternative to the Nazified church that had been established, that looked to the Aryan Christ. Absurd of course, but this perversion of Christianity did attract followers. Bonhoeffer was executed by the Nazis in 1945, just a few months before the Second World War ended. The film isn't always historically accurate, fails to grasp the man's essential pacifism, and the acting positively groans. But some of the reviews from Christian critics have been too harsh. The claim is that the movie is influenced by the conservative movement and has a political agenda, but I see no evidence of that. Nor do I think that people watch biopics and passively believe everything they see. There's a good chance that those who bother to watch the thing will then read the man's books and study him further, and that's surely what we want.

November 27

A friend sends me a video of an AI generated version of me giving a sermon. It's not perfect but not far off, and watching it gives me a very curious feeling. AI is developing so quickly that there are theologians and social commentators who worry that a new religion could develop around an extreme reverence for the technology.

The essence of religion is faith: a leap of commitment to something beyond direct knowledge and a love for that which we can never completely understand. Not so with AI, where a religious aura could develop around a nonexistent figure who appears on our screens and who seems all-knowing and all-understanding: all-knowing because it would have all of the information contained on the internet at its fingertips, all-understanding because your information will be there too — and often far more than you ever thought you had made public. "What is going to be created will effectively be a god," former Google engineer Anthony Levandowski has said. "It's not a god in the sense that it makes lightning or causes hurricanes. But if there is something a billion times smarter than the smartest human, what else are you going to call it?"

Is the deification of AI really so impossible? For the susceptible, instant communication with an entity representing a god, even God himself, could be transformative. The philosopher Blaise Pascal is said to have written that there is a god-shaped hole in each of us. Not sure if I agree, but the hunger to believe in something beyond the self is real. The *New York Times* has reported on the "pseudo-sacred industry" and the rise of so-called social divinity consultants who help introduce spiritual practices into tech companies. The massive decline in traditional religious adherence, combined with a craving for some kind of faith, has led many to embrace alien life, new-age offerings, and dangerous cults. For historian and scholar Yuval Noah Harari, AI could be even more alluring, especially if it starts generating scripture. Then the tool's oracular qualities can morph into a belief system that might spread and reshape society. "Religions throughout history claimed that their holy books were written by unknown human intelligence," Harari said at a recent science conference. "This was never true before. This could become true very, very quickly, with far-reaching consequences."

We don't have to wait for algorithms to conjure up a celestial figure. There's plenty AI could disrupt right now, such as revolutionizing the structure of a standard religious service. Whatever the denomination, the sermon is the major part of any such gathering, and I can tell you, as someone who writes and delivers them on a weekly basis, that it's a challenge to be original, fresh, and entertaining. At the current level being provided by AI tools like ChatGPT and anticipating what can be expected even in the near future, AI could create figures capable of injecting emotion, inflection, and sincerity into a homily and have quick access to the contents of every religious commentary there is. It could also find jokes and witticisms and be able to make it all seem bitingly relevant through its knowledge of current events. It will also possess the thumping advantage of immediacy. Rabbi Joshua Franklin, who leads the Jewish Centre of the Hamptons in East Hampton, posted on Vimeo a sermon written by ChatGPT he delivered last year. "You're clapping," Franklin told the congregation after he revealed the true author of the words he'd just spoken. "I'm deathly afraid."

What can't be provided, at least for the moment, is genuine personal contact and pastoral outreach and I'm trusting that this will never be properly copied. My belief as an Anglican priest is that I've been given authority by my bishop through what we refer to as the apostolic succession. That enables me to call on the Holy Spirit during the Eucharistic service when I pray over the bread and wine. A layperson can't do this, and certainly not a non-human system. But maybe the lack of association with any organized worship works in AI's favour. The technology would be a blank slate: an absence of malice, no history of harm.

To be sure, there are justifiable concerns about the technology's proneness to racist and discriminatory speech, shaped by the data it trains on. But we can imagine the opposite: an artificial entity that promotes itself as an expression of goodness and that, unlike religion down the ages, has never led Crusades, organized Inquisitions, or persecuted those with whom it differs. At least not yet.

Beyond all of this, however, is something more radical: the secular worship of AI itself. The idea, promoted by some techno-utopians, that such systems can solve any issue is maybe what we should really be fearing. Sam Altman, CEO of OpenAI, responsible for creating ChatGPT, said at a recent U.S. senate hearing that his company "was founded on the belief that artificial intelligence has the ability to improve nearly every aspect of our lives." I can't pretend that I'm not concerned.

November 28

"The only way to the truth," said the very Catholic U.S. novelist Flannery O'Connor, "is through Blasphemy." I quote her because this week in the British House of Commons, the Labour MP Tahir Ali asked, "Will the prime minister commit to introducing measures to prohibit the desecration of all religious texts and the prophets of the Abrahamic religions?" Sir Keir Starmer's response was so weak as to be put on life support. Rather than explaining that the right to question or mock religious faith was a fundamental right in any free society, and that even a hint of a blasphemy law was anathema to our way of life, the prime minister said, with consummate passivity, "Desecration is awful, and I think it should be condemned across the House. We are committed to tackling all forms of hatred and division including Islamophobia in all its forms." Starmer's supporters have described his answer as "reasonable under the circumstances," those circumstances presumably being that November is Islamophobia awareness month and that Tahir Ali's constituency is majority Muslim, a voting bloc the Labour Party can't afford to lose.

But is such desecration "awful"? I certainly oppose it, and as with Nazi book-burning, it can be a precursor to something far worse. But my concern is for people rather than objects, and the hideously ironic truth is that people are killed in the name of a similar religious fundamentalism that would introduce blasphemy laws. It's too glib to blame all of this on conservative Islam. Death for blasphemy has a history in ancient Judaism and not so ancient

Christianity. But today, the worst that would happen if a Bible were burnt would be a few angry demonstrators and a guest appearance on a comedy special lauding atheism.

I preach every week, argue the Christian case, take part in debates with non-believers who bring every cliché and insult they can to the debate. It warms my heart. Because the greatest danger to faith is indifference: people not opposing but simply ignoring. We drown in a sea of irrelevance. "If it works for you that's great, but don't bother me about it." I think I'd almost prefer it if they stamped on a prayer book! I realize that the Koran holds a unique place in Muslim theology and consciousness, and that behind textual destruction can be racism and hatred. But without freedom of speech there can be no authentic freedom of religion, which at its best demands an informed and often challenged acceptance. God forbid we ever lose the right to blaspheme.

December

December 3

Advent usually begins at the beginning of December, though can be as early as late November. Just to confuse people even more, the official church year begins — as I mentioned in the introduction — on the first Sunday of Advent, which is at the beginning of the month. Some of us wish each other "Happy New Year" but I'm not sure how many really mean it. This is the season before Christmas, and probably my favourite. We wait, we wonder, we anticipate, we prepare.

Charles Dickens's *A Christmas Carol* was published in 1843, when Britain was being transformed from a rural to an urban society with increased working hours, strains on families, and a wavering of traditions. Dickens wanted to emphasize the charitable nature of it all, to use it as a metaphor for social justice. The phrase "Merry Christmas" already existed, but Dickens was responsible for making it habitual, and while it sometimes snows at Christmas, the permanent linking of Christmas with snow is also quintessentially Dickensian — perhaps he wanted to evoke the idea of a washing away of dark, mid-Victorian inequality and exploitation.

Dickens was merely giving a reboot to a festival that had existed for centuries. Santa Claus or Father Christmas is a development of St. Nicholas, a Greek bishop from the fourth century, with a few hints of the Germanic god Wodan thrown in. The way he is depicted today is more Coca-Cola and Hollywood than that of the early church, but then, most good stories are collections of earlier legends. Decorating trees, kissing under mistletoe, carol singing, puddings, and the like have various origins — some ancient, others modern, all delightful. This is at least the third time that I've been asked by members of the church, and by journalists on radio or television, to explain the various ways we celebrate Christmas and to justify them. "Doesn't this mean that whole thing is just made up?" or "Isn't it more pagan than Christian?"

Let's consider the story behind these traditions — the one that it's fashionable to be cynical about. The early Christians didn't celebrate Christmas; Easter was the central event in their church calendar. Actually, it still is. In the fourth century, it was agreed to treat the birth of Christ as a holiday, but as scripture doesn't give any dates for the event, it had to be pretty much made up. That he was born during the winter is doubtful because sheep herding takes place in the spring, but nevertheless Pope Julius I opted for December 25, possibly to appeal to pagan converts who already observed the festival of Saturnalia in December. There were other factors, however. Many pre-Christian societies had long-established celebrations in December, and the winter solstice was important to northern Europeans who commemorated it with what they called the Yule, when logs would be put on the fire and those sitting around the flames would feast and drink. It was also one of the few times when meat was readily available because animals were slaughtered due to the difficulty of feeding them in the winter. Add to all this the Roman elite's affection for Mithra, the god of the unconquerable sun, whose birthday was celebrated on December 25, and we have a Christian holiday just waiting to happen.

But it's too glib, too convenient, to argue that the contrived nature of the date of the Christmas holiday somehow means that there was no nativity and thus that the entire Christian story is — sorry Charles — humbug. I agree that we need to be careful that we don't become submerged in tinselled nostalgia mingled with the self-prescribed absolute right of Christians to dominate the public square and dictate the private conscience, but that has nothing to do with Christmas.

As for followers of Jesus at Christmas time, they shouldn't be upset by irrelevant commercials for food, but by the fact that millions of people go without food altogether; it shouldn't be that Jesus's name is taken in vain but that His teachings are taken in vain; it shouldn't be that we don't say "Merry Christmas" as often as we did but that we seldom say "I forgive you," "You are loved," and "All are welcome in church." Regarding the once-ubiquitous question, "What would Jesus do?" the answer should probably be, "Tell everyone to grow up, re-read what the New Testament says, and then go and turn the world upside-down," not just at Christmas, but every day of the year.

I still watch *Frosty the Snowman* every Yuletide and love the fantasy of the season, but if I forget the authentic meaning of it all, I might as well genuflect to the great Santa in the sky.

I was doing some late Christmas shopping straight after church, still in my clericals and with my collar on. I saw a little girl, perhaps five or six years old, staring at me. Then she looked up at her mum and asked, "Mum, is he Santa?" Her mother, briefly glancing up at me, obviously busy, nonchalantly replied, "No darling, he's the other one." I rather like the idea of being the other one.

Santa Claus may be a de-Christianized version of St. Nicholas, but he is also the personification of love for innocence and goodness, and in him, magic abounds. These things are there for a purpose, to remind a world that too easily forgets that altruism and brotherly love are what genuinely matter. G.K. Chesterton wrote a beautiful piece about how medieval Englishmen believed their farm animals would bow as one at a hidden, precise time on Christmas night to show their reverence for the Son of God. True or not, it's a lovely image; how tragic that the same contemporary culture that embraces without question every ghoulish fad also chuckles at any ancient tale that boasts God and Jesus. Chesterton also wrote a poem called "The Donkey."

> When fishes flew and forests walked
> And figs grew upon thorn,
> Some moment when the moon was blood
> Then surely I was born.
>
> With monstrous head and sickening cry
> And ears like errant wings,
> The devil's walking parody
> On all four-footed things.
>
> The tattered outlaw of the earth,
> Of ancient crooked will;
> Starve, scourge, deride me: I am dumb,
> I keep my secret still.
>
> Fools! For I also had my hour;
> One far fierce hour and sweet:
> There was a shout about my ears,
> And palms before my feet.

It was Chesterton who brought me to Canada, because it was at a G.K. Chesterton conference in Toronto in 1986 that I met the woman I'd marry. I re-read the poem every Christmas Day and thank him with all I have.

In my secular, half-Jewish family, Christmas was always eagerly anticipated: the old plastic tree brought down from the attic, school holidays, lots of excitement, food, gifts, and fun. All I knew was that Father Christmas was munificent if judgmental, Oliver Cromwell once stole our Christmas puddings (if you don't know the story, Google is your friend), and the nice people next door always came home uncharacteristically late on Christmas Eve. I'm now ambivalent about Cromwell, have lost touch with our churchgoing neighbours, but still think Santa is far too intolerant of the naughty. I also believe that God became incarnate as a baby two thousand years ago, that he preached a revolutionary doctrine of love, grace, forgiveness, and salvation, and that the Christmas story is authentic and transforming.

I've become convinced that the most extraordinary things happen each Christmas season. That might be due to a rare collective goodwill, the product of holiday euphoria, family gatherings, giving and getting, and reruns of *It's a Wonderful Life* and *A Christmas Carol*, but I feel there's something more, and I say this not as some naive dreamer but as someone who has covered brutal wars and unforgiving sectarian violence. In other words, I'm not easily duped.

An elderly parishioner named Jackie died during this Advent and Christmas season. Her death had been anticipated, so I saw her several times before she passed. I wasn't there when she died but arrived shortly afterwards, and prayed over her with her husband, George. But there's more to the story. Jackie and her husband of fifty-five years didn't have any children, there was little immediate family, and their friends had almost all predeceased them. This happens a lot with older people, and the consequent loneliness is one of society's unacknowledged terrors. When I left George mid-evening, I promised I'd call him and gave him my direct number. I telephoned him the next day to see how he was. There was a cacophony of happy noise in the background. The church knew what had happened and in the space of a few hours had organized a schedule of visits, when groups of people, some of them teenagers, would knock on his door with food and drink and throw miniature parties in honour of Jackie. And in honour of the coming Christmas. All of the days leading up to Christmas were covered and, as one of the leaders said to me, "by that time we'll all be good friends and there won't be any need for a diary." They took care of the "sadmin" (what we call the endless and distressing paperwork after a death) and made sure George was never without someone to speak to. The pain would never pass, of course, and grieving is a long-term process, but this was priceless.

December 7

Winter is a dying time but nature is beautiful in its retreat, still defending itself, preparing for the stings and the storms and the snow. It's also a time for people to reconsider and revaluate, to prepare for the new year. That idea of rebirth is, I'm told, why Derek has come to see me. He's gay, has always known he's gay, and because of that has left the church. He emailed me last week and now we meet in person. "I've read your book, and I know the arguments for the Christian acceptance of people like me," he says. "But what about the people in the pews, what will they think of me? I want to come back, I've never abandoned my faith in Jesus, but I'm not sure I want to hang out with Christians."

I say that the Church of England, divided over the issue for many years, now performs officially sanctioned blessings of same-sex partnerships. I explain that Pope Francis has announced that Catholic priests would be allowed to do something similar (although his ruling was more qualified than that of the Church of England) but that these blessings weren't to be performed within a church ritual or liturgy and the decision to perform them would be left to "the prudent and fatherly discernment of ordained ministers." But there's much more to it than that. Yes, of course he'd be welcome and welcomed; he wouldn't be the only gay person in the church, and for many clergy, perhaps most in the Anglican church, this wasn't an issue any longer and hadn't been in a while. When we said that we were affirming, I told him, we meant it from our very souls.

I understand those Christians who cannot accept gay relationships, and I was there once. I think that they're wrong, but I have to try to reach them kindly. But I'm straight and this isn't personal for me the way it is with Derek and so many like him. If those opposed to equal marriage and the Christian embrace of LGBTQ2S people could see the damage they've caused, the broken families, the rejected children, maybe they'd change their minds. Oh, how I hope I'm right.

December 9

Netflix has released its long-promised film on the life of the Virgin Mary. It's not that bad but not very good either. Why bother? Because Christmas is coming and the streaming services have to fill up with seasonal movies.

The film is nothing too heretical: there's an over-the-top but still meaty portrayal of Herod by Sir Anthony Hopkins, and rather convincing scenery — most Biblical epics are now filmed in Morocco. Some crucial parts of the Christmas story are omitted for no apparent reason, and some imagined scenes have been added that do nothing to clarify or magnify. The lead actress is competent enough and certainly looks the part, probably because twenty-two-year-old Noa Cohen is Israeli.

And here's why people are talking about the thing and why there are protests and calls to boycott it. The terrible fate of Gaza is filling our screens, and there's an understandable anguish of Palestinians, so there have been roars that the lead role should have been given to a Palestinian actress.

Director Daniel John Caruso replied that "it was important to us that Mary, along with most of our primary cast, be selected from Israel to ensure authenticity." Frankly, I'm not overly concerned with the casting, although to be fair I'd challenge you to find many Jewish, let alone Israeli, actors who've ever played Mary, Jesus, or any of the disciples on the screen. For many years the leads in Biblical movies looked more Scandinavian than Jewish. More perniciously, for centuries European art emphasized the non-Jewish appearance of Jesus and the Jewishness of Judas. I so bloody wish this subject would go away.

December 10

It's fascinating how some authors seem to enjoy fashion while others are left behind by it. George MacDonald was born on December 10, 1824, and while not an official saint, his influence on many of the most important Christian authors in modern history may well qualify him as one. C.S. Lewis wrote, "I know hardly any other writer who seems to be closer, or more continuously close, to the Spirit of Christ Himself. I have never concealed the fact that I regarded him as my master; indeed, I fancy I have never written a book in which I did not quote from him." G.K. Chesterton described him as "an elemental figure, a man unconnected with any particular age, a character in one of his own fairy tales, a true mystic to whom the supernatural was natural."

The author of *Phantastes*, *The Princess and the Goblin*, *At the Back of the North Wind*, *The Diary of an Old Soul*, and *Lilith* was born in Huntly, Aberdeenshire, to a family with deep Highland ancestry. He was awarded a bursary to the University of Aberdeen, but to supplement his income, he catalogued books in a castle library, and it was there that he was introduced to German fairy tales. After university he moved to London, where he worked as a tutor before being ordained and ministering at Trinity Congregational Church in Arundel, West Sussex. Never a traditional Calvinist, his embrace of Jesus's invincible love for everybody and not just the predestined few made him unpopular. The church punished him by halving his salary. He was married by this time, and he and his wife would eventually have eleven children. A ministerial income, let alone half of one, was never going to be sufficient. Influenced by those German fairy tales he'd encountered, he began to write. He was also mixing in literary circles and his home — described as a place of "light and warmth" — attracted an authorial set. The educational reformer and philanthropist Anne Milbanke, wife of Lord Byron, became a frequent guest, as did Lewis Carroll, whom MacDonald encouraged to publish the Alice stories.

This was so distant from the strict, almost fundamentalist, Protestantism of MacDonald's former days. His wider, more inclusive Christian theology combined with an embrace of fantasy literature led in 1858 to his publishing the book *Phantastes: A Faerie Romance for Men and Women. Anodos*, "pathless" in Greek, enters a dream world where he searches for his ideal of beauty while resisting various temptations and challenges. "My soul was like a summer evening, after a heavy fall of rain," he wrote, "when the drops are yet glistening on the trees in the last rays of the down-going sun, and the wind of the twilight has begun to blow." A later edition would be illustrated by the Pre-Raphaelite painter Arthur Hughes.

He would write more than fifty works of fiction, collections of sermons, and children's stories, but was never sufficiently successful to keep his family financially secure. In 1877, partly through the influence of admiring friends, he was given a Civil List pension.

His questioning of orthodox interpretations of damnation and hell, his mingling of Germanic and North European folklore with Christian theology, and his ability to intellectually legitimize fantasy and innocent wonder may not have achieved Dickensian popularity, but if we read anything by Lewis or Tolkien, or even by modern, secular, science-fiction writers, his legacy is inescapable. As a Christian he was perceptive and provocative. "It may be an infinitely less evil to murder a man than to refuse to forgive him. The former may be the act of a moment of passion: the latter is the heart's choice." And "If God were not only to hear our prayers, as he does ever and always, but to answer them as we want them answered, he would not be God our Saviour but the ministering genius of our destruction." My wife is a devotee of the man, and many years ago I bought her a letter of his with his signature at the bottom, which is framed and still hangs in her study.

December 13

Early morning weekday services are never well attended, even in many of the world's great cathedrals let alone a suburban church. They attract a diverse group, some regulars, and some passersby; Elsie was one of the regulars. Nobody was sure if that was actually her name, but everybody knew her. She'd arrive seconds before the service began and rush out as soon as it was over. She always carried a plastic bag bulging with goodness knows what, wore the same heavy crimson coat, whatever the weather, and danced a little jig when the priest consecrated the host. Elsie was as much a fixture as the crucifix behind the altar.

Then, one Christmas she wasn't there. This was unusual because Elsie was there every day, rain, snow, or sun. At the end of the service the priest asked us to remain for a moment, and he then told us that Elsie had died in the early hours. We were all invited to her funeral. I went along not because I knew the woman beyond the occasional smile but because I assumed hardly anybody would be there. It was packed. I recognized some of the morning regulars but not the hundred or so other mourners, from every background imaginable.

It was only after the funeral that I discovered Elsie's story. How this child of a wealthy family had lived in a tiny apartment and spent all her inheritance helping people in need, how she spent her days walking around feeding people on the street and chatting and listening to them. She'd made herself smaller so they could be larger and given her entire life to the service of others. She'd suffered with chronic pain most of her adult years but told her priest she was happy and that her only wish was to die at Christmas time, when we celebrate the birth of her saviour.

December 14

How can any Christian not try to emulate Jesus's embrace of the poor, the rejected, the marginalized, and the oppressed? The answer is that they can't, if they're serious about it all. We can argue about theology, history, and translation all day long, but the central point of the life that would be led by the baby born two thousand years ago is that we have to love one another. So if you think being Christian is easy, you've been listening to the wrong people. God forgive them, there are lots of "wrong people" when it comes to the church. The baby whose birth we are soon to celebrate became a man who proposed a new paradigm, a new relationship between people, a new way of being, living, and doing. What he also told us was that individual change was possible and that we're all capable of being "born again."

If anybody understood the human capacity to doubt and hate, it was Jesus, whose death on a cross saw the temporary triumph of darkness and despair. The world is as divided and bloody as it's ever been, and in some ways the potential for pain and terror is greater than ever. That makes Christmas and everything for which it stands not less but more relevant. The Christian faith isn't naive or childish, and a mature understanding of the Gospels should lead us to know precisely how difficult life can be. But if we surrender the fight for justice, equality, peace, hope, and love, then we fail God and fail that baby whose birth changed everything. In my better moments that reality washes over me and makes me complete.

December 17

It looks like Justin Trudeau has very little time left as prime minister. He's been far from perfect, and there were minor scandals, personal mistakes, and a pride that prevented him from resigning a year or so ago. But if we consider his nine years in office calmly and objectively, he was in many ways one of the more Christian premiers in the democratic world. I say this because many Christians denounce the man as an enemy of the faith and someone who has abandoned the community. Good Lord, it was as if he'd slaughtered every second bishop he came across!

Their opposition is theological shorthand, of course. They detest him because he led a country that allows abortion and enshrines women's rights, champions same-sex marriage and gay equality, has legalized assisted dying, and closed churches during the deadly Covid-19 pandemic. Abortion rights and equal marriage were, in fact, part of Canadian life long before Trudeau came on the scene, although he was prime minister in 2016 when Medical Assistance in Dying, or MAID, was introduced. In his defence, many of us failed to see how damaging this decision would eventually be.

As for closing churches during Covid-19, the policy was supported by the leadership of the vast majority of denominations, including the Roman Catholic Church in a country that is almost 30 percent Catholic. The measure saved lives, as did Trudeau's remarkably speedy procurement of vaccines at a time when they were frighteningly scarce. He also provided financial support for businesses and individuals during the shutdown.

Outside of the pandemic, he accepted and resettled thousands of Syrian refugees, introduced numerous climate justice measures, worked for affordable public daycare, supported human rights abroad, and pursued a balanced policy when advocating for peace in the Middle East. He appointed a cabinet that was 50 percent female, though his repeated appointments made women the majority on the Supreme Court for the first time in Canadian history. He acted effectively on reconciliation with Canada's Indigenous people. He legalized cannabis so as to prevent people, especially the young, from receiving unnecessary criminal records, and stood up to and was impressively gracious in dealing with abusive personal and family attacks that were staggering in their intensity.

So, whatever one thinks of the man, it's difficult to see him as a vehement anti-Christian. It's true that a number of churches were subject to arson attacks after more cases of the church's appalling treatment of native children were revealed, and while Trudeau could have arguably spoken out more firmly, he can hardly be blamed for these crimes. On a personal level, some of the antipoverty and welfare programs initiated by the Trudeau government have made my work a great deal easier. There is still, however, so much more to be done.

Part of the raw dislike of Trudeau is because of his father, Pierre, who genuinely did change Canada, some claiming that he enabled it to become a permissive and non-Christian country. That assumes, of course, that Christianity and modern, liberal values are somehow mutually exclusive. I'd argue the contrary, and that Trudeau the father and the son rooted their ideology in a Christian, specifically Roman Catholic, commitment to equality, dignity, and justice.

The next government is likely to be Conservative and will almost certainly tighten borders, reduce or remove environmental protection taxes, attack public broadcasting, question economic redistribution policies, abandon various progressive ideals, and strengthen Canada's links with the Trump presidency. But it will probably speak of Christian values, mention God and prayer a great deal, and wish people Merry Christmas, and because of these practices be seen as a firm defender of Christianity. I do wonder if the church always knows who its real friends and allies are.

December 20

Sometimes, laughter is essential, even if it's misplaced laughter. Today a man started banging on the church doors. He was wearing a hospital gown and still had his wristband on; our local hospital is only a fifteen-minute walk away. I offered him food and drink, but he wasn't interested. It was difficult to understand what he wanted so I just listened. He then wandered off, removing the rest of his clothes. The police eventually arrived, making it clear that they knew the guy. "Oh yeah, he's an old friend," said a policewoman to me. "We'll do what we can but it's not much. Last time we had to deal with him he told me how beautiful I was and asked if I'd take him home with me. I told him I was married. He said that was okay because he was very broad-minded."

December 21

Winter is the time for funerals. I've never researched the statistics, but it does seem to be that way. If it's true, it could be that along with people's acceptance of the end of the year, they still wish to see just one more Christmas before the end. Winter funerals are not always as sombre as you'd think. At one, a middle-aged man seemed to be in bad shape and was crying after the service was over. I approached him, said I was available if there was anything I could do for him and that Jim — the deceased — had been a good man. "Jim," he replied. "I don't know any Jim. I'm here for Billy." He'd come to the wrong funeral! I assumed he'd dry his eyes and leave, but no. He said, "Well, as long as I'm here I might as well have a good cry anyway."

More challenging was the mourner who recognized me from my days on television and asked if he could take a selfie with me. That was awkward. If I refused and told him that this wasn't really the time and place, he might have become upset or considered me a snob. On the other hand, he might have been in much deeper grief than it appeared, and the interaction might have helped him. Would other people notice, what would they think of me? In the end I agreed, trying hard to put on my concerned but not unfriendly face for the photo, which probably looked like I had gas.

I've taken a funeral for a Muslim man who attended our church's community lunches. I asked the funeral home repeatedly if the family wanted a Christian priest, but they were insistent. I can't imagine that he was very religious; what mattered was that he'd built up a relationship with a welcoming and inclusive community.

The funeral for Mary's husband was formal and neat but lacked the emotion and tenderness I usually see. After the sandwiches and little cakes — the food at funerals is often surprisingly good — Mary asked me to sit down with her. "You know, I never really loved him. Perhaps at the beginning, but that was more likely infatuation. But pretty soon after that it was flat, ordinary, day-to-day. He provided for us, for me and the children, and he was kind in his own way, never especially unpleasant and certainly never violent or abusive, but I just didn't love him." Best to say nothing at these times, and it was obvious that she hadn't finished. "I suppose that if I'd been younger, you know kids these days, I'd have left him. But it seemed wrong, unfair. He was trying his best, the children would have been devastated, and my friends and family would have been angry with me. So, I did my duty, really. Was I wrong, Father; was I wrong?"

The silence was broken by one of the caterers saying goodbye. Then I said to Mary that only she knew the answer, not me. She sacrificed for a good person, a good man, and for her children. That could never be wrong, but she also sacrificed her own happiness, and that was for her to decide on. The main thing, I continued, was that she made the most of the years she had left. I saw that there were tears in her eyes. Not the crying I'm so used to but something else. She began to nod her head, then thanked me more than what I thought I deserved and left. I never heard from her again until a year later when she telephoned me and asked if I'd bless her partnership with a "gentleman" she'd met who had lost his wife. They weren't getting married, she explained, because they thought they were too old for that and the first time around had been enough. At which I laughed a little. They intended to be, she continued, partners and best friends and companions for the years they had left.

December 22

We're frightened of death and that's entirely understandable. Frightened of losing those we love and of our own departure. Of not being here. In my experience, Jews and Irish Catholics cope best with mourning. Sitting Shiva provides time for reflection and support. And food, which is not a bad combination. The wake injects a sense of joy, or something approaching it, into a time soaked in pain. Remembering the good, the fun, and the love in the person who has died. If a couple of drinks are consumed, so much the better. Humour, believe it or not, helps, and honesty is vital. Being compassionate and being patronizing aren't the same thing, and just because someone is grieving doesn't mean they've suddenly become less intelligent or aware. Never talk down to someone who is in pain. Equality at a time of suffering can work wonders. I genuinely believe that this is only the land of shadows and real life hasn't begun yet, but I couch those words in the reality of the room. The worst thing a priest can do is to offer platitudes.

Can I rationalize pain and loss? Not really. Bad things happen to good people. What I can and do say is that in my mind, in my faith, Jesus has been there before us, suffered before us and suffered for us. In a divine leap of solidarity, he felt what we now feel. The most important thing any of us can do is simply to be present. Be there, accept the anger, and don't try to explain what can't be explained, certainly not when wounds are bleeding raw and open. Also, consider the context. Those mourning the death of elderly parents are often married and have families around them, and there's something natural and in a way more acceptable about that situation. Those who have lost spouses, at any age, are in a much darker place. Relish life's every moment, remind those close to you of your love, forgive until it hurts, and try to ignore the pointless noise that so surrounds us in order to concentrate on the important things.

December 24

Today is my favourite day of the year and always has been. There's a layer of excitement in the air, something between a rosy mist and a ray of sunshine, or is it an unexpected scent? I take communion home to people, make telephone calls, and then take one of our numerous evening services. It's as though the door to the eternal is more open than usual. My friend Malcolm Guite is a priest in the Church of England and a gifted poet. His "A Tale of Two Gardens" contains the following lines:

> He found us where we hid from him
> He clothed us in his grace
> But still we turned our backs on him
> And would not see his face.
>
> So now he comes to us again
> Not as a Lord most high
> But weak and helpless as we are
> That we might hear him cry.
>
> And he who clothed us in our need
> Lies naked in the straw
> That we might wrap him in our rags
> Whom once we fled in awe.

Clothed us in our need. That's it, that's the story.

December 25

Christmas Day. The first Christmas I vividly remember is that of 1965 when I was six years old. My entire life seemed bathed in joy and innocence. There wasn't much money in my family but there were love, hugs, and trust abounding. My school was a short walk from where I lived, I felt safe there, and at the end of each day our teacher would read books to us. Christmas was close, so she'd decided on *The Lion, the Witch and the Wardrobe* by C.S. Lewis. The teacher's voice was like velvet, I was spellbound, and the story of children in a strange, magical land, of battles, of talking animals, and even of Father Christmas enthralled me. My family wasn't Christian, I was too young to grasp the Christian imagery in the book, but I knew I had to find out more.

My mum met me when school ended at 4:00 p.m. and all I could talk about was this extraordinary book. I wasn't sure of the title but insisted to my poor mother that I had to have a copy. She never learnt to drive and anyway we didn't own a car at the time, so she took the bus to the closest bookstore and managed to find a copy. I couldn't have understood all the words, but I know I stayed up all night looking at them, and the illustrations, and that when Christmas came a few days later it seemed different, more alive, more special than ever.

Something was planted in those days, something that would take many years to mature and blossom. But today, I look around and see so much suffering. Jesus didn't promise a comfortable life and, if anything, predicted hard times for those who would be his followers, and it's always amused me when I'm told that Christianity is for the weak or provides an escape from reality. In fact, the contrary is true. To follow he who was born at Christmas is to open our arms and hearts to all those who weep and need our help. To travel where others will not go and speak for those who have no voice. The closest we ever come to God is when we're with another person. Even so, the pain is hard to accept. At Christmas the need to be there for those hurting is all the greater because the lonely, grieving, and sick feel especially isolated. The warm glow of friends and family is an icy wind for those without either. Embrace the prejudice of love. Prejudge people as souls, made in the image of God, full of goodness and beauty. We'll sometimes be let down, but if we haven't realized that reality as followers of Jesus, we haven't been paying attention.

Fast forward forty-five years and my mother is in a hospital bed. She's dying, ravaged by the hideous swine of dementia, and unable to speak or react. I ask God for answers, remembering that he knows what I feel because he too has suffered. It began with a cradle but ended with a cross. I sit by mum's bed and read to her. Not from the Bible or a prayer book, because mum wasn't religious and wasn't a Christian. No, I read her *The Lion, the Witch and the Wardrobe.* Well of course I do. And I read it to myself once again this Christmas, with tears in my eyes.

December 31

So ends the year. I will be sixty-six years old in two weeks, so there are far fewer years in front of me than behind me. As the year comes to end, I wonder how many diaries there will be in the future. But I take so much comfort in my four children growing further in their beautiful maturity, and in their kindness and goodness and charm. See my grandson, and perhaps grandchildren, play and laugh, and see their wonder at what the world shows them. I thank God for my vocation, and for my marriage.

It's 11:30 p.m. and my wife and I look at each other and realize that we're not going to stay awake until midnight. Let's open the sparkling wine early and call it a night. We have a drink, save the rest for the first day of the new year, wish one another a happy new year, hug, and then go to bed. But no. My phone rings. It's someone from church who is on her own for the new year for the first time after her husband died. She's very apologetic, knows it's late, but there was nobody else to speak to. Would I chat for a while just to keep her company? My pleasure, I say; my privilege. By the time our conversation ends, a new year has begun. Just the way it should do.

About the Author

Michael Coren is a broadcaster, columnist, and speaker. He hosted a daily television show for fifteen years for which he won numerous awards. Michael is a columnist for the *Toronto Star* and a frequent contributor to *The Globe and Mail*, TVO, and *The Walrus* in Canada, and *The New Statesman*, *The Times*, *The Telegraph*, *The Oldie*, and *Church Times* in Britain. He is the bestselling author of twenty books, including biographies of G.K. Chesterton, H.G. Wells, Arthur Conan Doyle, J.R.R. Tolkien, and C.S. Lewis, and has contributed to the *Dictionary of National Biography* and several other anthologies. Michael has published in many countries and in more than a dozen languages. In 2005, he won the Edward R. Murrow Award for Radio Broadcasting; in 2006, the RTDNA Canada Radio Broadcasting Award; in 2007, the Communicator Award in Hollywood; and in 2008, the Omni Award for his television show. In 2012, he was awarded the Queen's Jubilee Medal for services to media. Michael is a priest in the Anglican Church of Canada.